B305

DATE DUE FEB 0 4

5-11-04			
6-22-04			
8-18-04			
10-27-04			
9-1-05			
GAYLORD			PRINTED IN U.S.A.

RANDOM HOUSE
HOUSE

LARGE
PRINT

BRINKLEY'S BEAT

BRINKLEY'S BEAT

◆

People, Places, and Events
That Shaped My Time

DAVID BRINKLEY

R A N D O M   H O U S E
L A R G E   P R I N T

*The Library of Congress has established
a Cataloging-in-Publication record for this title*

0-375-43222-1

www.randomlargeprint.com

FIRST LARGE PRINT EDITION

10   9   8   7   6   5   4   3   2   1

This Large Print edition published in
accord with the standards of the
N.A.V.H.

To my grandchildren:
Katie, Elly, Charlotte, Maeve,
and those to come

Contents

Preface

Here I am. I am sitting on a hard bench in the county recorder's courtroom in Wilmington, North Carolina, in about 1938, where I am a junior reporter, waiting in the thin, pale hope that something, anything happening here in court this morning might be worth a few lines I can write for that afternoon's *Star-News*. Usually, nothing here is any more interesting or picturesque than the case being considered today: a defendant, a retired carpenter, being tried on charges of public drunkenness and urinating on the sidewalk. Nevertheless, the courtroom is crowded this and every morning with older and middle-aged men, nearly all of them dressed in cotton pants and white shirts buttoned up to the neck with no necktie, here five days a week for the morning's free entertainment. While they waited, many of them lit Hav-A-Tampa nickel cigars, pulled them out of their wrapping, tied the cellophane in a knot, and threw it toward the county-issue brass spittoon, nearly always missing. The retired carpenter was found guilty of public drunkenness and indecent exposure and sentenced to a week on the county farm a mile or two outside of town, where non-dangerous prisoners were held; they were required to serve their sentences doing farm work, their produce, mostly cabbage, being used to feed the inmates.

This was a more or less normal day's work for the judge, known as the recorder in ancient English terminology, and his was the first hearing for petty criminals and routine drunks and violators of the traffic rules, mostly the speed limits. Only once did one of these make a few lines in my newspaper. A man was accused of driving sixty-five miles an hour on the Carolina Beach Road where the speed limit was fifty. He pleaded not guilty, saying his car, a ten-year-old Essex, would not even go sixty-five, and so he could not be guilty. The only witness was a motorcycle policeman who said he clocked him at sixty-five. The judge— mainly out of boredom, I thought—called for some kind of evidence. Would anyone in the court volunteer to drive the Essex while the policeman followed him on his motorcycle and carefully clocked his speed?

Nobody else volunteered and so I did, seeing an amusing little story. I drove out the same road and pushed the Essex to its limit while the policeman followed on his motorcycle. When the Essex, groaning and straining and rattling, passed seventy-five miles an hour, the policeman signaled with his headlight that the test was done and we returned to court. It cost the defendant a fifteen-dollar fine. It cost me a stern lecture from Lamont Smith, the paper's editor, that it was a neat little story but even so my job was to report the news, not to make it.

When people ask me how I got started in journalism, I often tell them about the story that got me my first job on the *Star-News*. I was hanging around the paper as a stringer, and I answered the phone to hear a woman on North Fifth Street bubbling with what she thought was news. "I have a century plant my grandfather bought long ago and it's going to bloom Tuesday night and I thought the paper would like to know about it." A century plant is a lily that blooms at intervals of between five and a hundred years, according to the encyclopedia I had at the time, but no one I knew had ever seen one. I put a one-inch item in the paper quoting her. The woman was soon flooded with phone calls from local residents asking if they could come to see this great event, a century plant in bloom, and so on.

When Tuesday night arrived, North Fifth Street was choked with traffic. Vendors were selling orange and grape Popsicles for the children. People on the street complained of the strangers at their doors asking to use their bathrooms. The fire department sent a truck with a floodlight to light up the street. The century plant, meanwhile, sat on the front porch in a ceramic pot, looking like a small broom handle with no branches and no leaves. I watched all this and wondered who would be blamed when it turned out nothing happened. Nothing did, but no one seemed to care. They were having too good a time enjoying the carnival that this nonevent had created. Or at least almost no one cared. A short, gray-haired man in khaki pants and a blue work shirt, a flat Prince Albert pipe tobacco can in the breast pocket, said to nobody in particular, "Look at all the trash they're leaving in the street. Popsicle sticks all over! The city has to clean this up! What's all this mess costing the taxpayers?" He was still carrying on when I left for the office. I turned in a story not about the century plant, but about the madness on North Fifth Street. Lamont Smith liked it enough to give me a full-time job.

I like to tell that story because it seems to me to illustrate something that characterized my career in journalism. One of the words people often used to describe me when I first became well known in the late 1950s was "wry," not a word much used anymore—or even then. Its literal definition is "lopsided," "misdirected," "ironic," or "humorous." I suppose I was sometimes all those things. I was always attracted to the comical, even the ridiculous. And although much of what I covered over the years was serious, and even tragic, I tried never to lose sight of the pretension and folly that was always there, even in the gravest situations. In the troubled times in which I have finished this book, I think it's still important to be a little detached, to keep an eye out for the foolish and the ridiculous, and to avoid accepting everything at face value. That's what most of the stories in this book try to do, and it's part of what I tried to do during my more than fifty years in broadcasting.

Acknowledgments

The people I should really thank for helping me with this book are all the wonderful men and women who worked with me over the years at NBC and ABC and made it possible for me to cover the stories that I've tried to recall here. But there are too many of them to list, so I'll thank by name just a few who helped me with the book itself. Thad Russell and Lynn Robeson did wonderful research, which was invaluable in helping compensate for my own selective memory. My agent, Peter Matson, helped me get started on this project, and my editor at Knopf, Ash Green, was, as always, a patient, perceptive, and supportive partner. My children—Alan, Joel, John, and Alexis—all talked with me about some of the things I describe in the book and helped me reconstruct events they too witnessed or heard about. My wife, Susan, was, as she has always been, my greatest helper and supporter.

BRINKLEY'S BEAT

PEOPLE

Theodore Bilbo

I arrived in Washington in 1943, when the city was fast becoming a crowded, bustling war capital—filled with clerks and business-men and diplomats and exiled foreign lead-ers. But my life was pretty simple: riding the segregated trolleys downtown to work at the NBC offices in the old Trans-Lux building on Fourteenth Street; living in rented rooms in private houses—the only housing available at any price—and having to deal with cranky landlords and landladies who constantly posted on the walls new rules of behavior and reminders of the need for neatness in the bathrooms. I had come to Washington from the South, and despite the new bustle, it had a very familiar feeling. It was sleepy, often slow-moving, inbred, and thoroughly segregated.

Local Washington, through presidents, wars, and depressions, had settled into an acceptance of George Washington's poor choice of location in a sprawling, slow-moving Southern city. People from real cities—New York, Chicago, Boston, cities with factories and immigrants and sub-ways—thought it astonishing. There were few restaurants offering anything not fried in deep fat. On Connecticut Avenue there was a place called Old New Orleans featuring in its front display window a large, plump black woman wearing a long gingham dress and a red bandanna on her head and sitting in a rocking chair, rocking by the hour—the restaurant's trademark. Only a river's breadth away lay the old Confederacy. Robert E. Lee's house, Arlington, still stood on the opposite bank. The speaker of the House of Representatives, Sam Rayburn of Bonham, Texas, had not one but five pictures of Lee on his office wall, symmetrically arranged and all facing south. For whites as for blacks, Washington was southern. Capital of the United States, yes, but southern in manner, style, and appearance and southern in climate and culture.

I lived in Washington for fifty-five years after that, and saw it change a great deal before I left. But the image that has always stayed with me is of the quiet town I visited first with my mother in the 1930s, when we stayed at the old Hotel Harrington downtown, and of the only slightly noisier town I found when I moved there in the early 1940s.

To me, as a sometime Capitol Hill reporter, the antiquated character of the city was most visible in Congress, which was still carrying on in the manner of a fading aristocracy, in a setting of marble stairways, horsehair sofas, polished brass spittoons, snuffboxes on the senators' desks, potted palms, Oriental rugs, leather chairs, and Havana cigars. There were even a few members still affecting frock coats, wing collars, and black string ties. Through the 1930s, it was a gentlemen's club with but one woman senator—Hattie Caraway of Arkansas, who sat in the chamber every day knitting, listening, and saying nothing.

"People don't give a damn what the average Senator or Congressman says," the columnist Raymond Clapper wrote. "The reason they don't care is that they know what you hear in Congress is 99 per cent tripe, ignorance and demagoguery and not to be relied on." Clapper's description applied to many politicians on Capitol Hill, but it fit no one better than a man from Mississippi, one of the most extraordinary and preposterous figures I ever encountered in my many years as a Washington reporter.

United States Senator Theodore Gilmore Bilbo (known at home as "The Man") was somewhere between five feet and five feet six inches tall. He was a vain man, often described as a "strutting peacock," and he refused to reveal his exact height. But one Mississippian who helped vote him into the Senate said, "When Theo Bilbo is on the stump, he's seven feet ten inches tall," which gives some idea of Bilbo's talent as an orator, a talent he used freely in getting himself elected state senator, lieutenant governor, governor, and finally U.S. senator for two terms. Bilbo led a charmed political life, surviving scandal, imprisonment, defeat, and outrage, and climbing higher and higher all the time. In the 1940s, when he sat in the Senate during the greatest war in history, even colleagues who had been sharing the chamber with him for over a decade sometimes found it hard to believe that someone like him could really be there.

Bilbo, the youngest of ten children, was born in 1877 on a farm in the wire-grass country of Mississippi, six miles from the railroad station at Poplarville. It was an area of the state with little cotton and not many blacks; an area where slavery had not much taken root and where loyalty to the Confederacy had been relatively weak. People from around Poplarville had a lively resentment of the planter aristocracy and a belief that ordinary people were getting a raw deal from the government and the corporations. Like many poor whites, they also had a real contempt for black people—mostly because they needed someone they could feel superior to.

In Bilbo's family, as in most others in the area, money was not plentiful. He went to school only by paying his own expenses. Between terms at Peabody College and Vanderbilt University, where he won a law degree, he sandwiched work as a "news butcher" on southern trains. While selling bananas and newspapers up and down lurching train aisles, he learned phrenology, a system by which some people thought they could determine character from head shapes. "During those days," he said, "I earned as much as $250 a month." He claimed he could look at a passenger's head and determine the quickest and best way to separate him from his money.

After college, Bilbo became a traveling Sunday school organizer and won a preacher's license as a reward for secretarial services at Baptist institutions. Those who heard him said he could preach a thumping sermon on the regular minister's day off. Those who heard his speeches in later years didn't doubt it.

He first ran for office, county court clerk, at the age of twenty-two and lost by ninety-six votes. At thirty he was back again, seeking a $250-a-year job as state senator. He tore into that campaign furiously, rode his father's horse two thousand miles, and took his message to the people. They liked it and elected him by a big majority.

The story of Bilbo and that first term in the legislature became famous in Mississippi, and there have been almost as many versions as tellers. It involves a well-documented charge of bribery, impeachment proceedings, and a resolution calling him "unfit to sit with honest, upright men in a respectable legislative body." He was saved from impeachment by one vote and forever after blamed the impeachment attempt on the fat cats trying to get rid of him before he got rid of them.

Bilbo took the stump again four years later and won election as lieutenant governor. His first official act was to remove the "unfit" resolution from the records. The next four years were uneventful, except for another bribery charge and another acquittal. Bilbo then told the voters he wanted to be governor. They obliged him in 1915, burnishing the already growing legend of his political indestructibility. A defeated opponent once said, "The lower you push Theo Bilbo, the higher he bounces back."

As governor, in one uproarious day, Bilbo fired the presidents of the University of Mississippi, the State College for Women, and the A and M College. On the same day he fired 179 professors and teachers. For chancellor of the university system he named a real-estate salesman who held no degree. The Mississippi Power and Light Company's advertising manager was made president of A and M. For a University Administration Board, he chose two dentists, one bank cashier, one doctor, and three lawyers. When Bilbo was criticized for tampering with the schools, his only answer was "Things have come to a hell of a pass when a man can't wallop his own jackass."

Bilbo was not a particularly handsome man. But he didn't seem to know it, and neither, apparently, did most of the people in Mississippi who came to hear him. He had a flair for showmanship, particularly in his wardrobe. He stocked up on pinkish shirts, flaming red neckties, red suspenders, and red handkerchiefs. (At night he wore red pajamas.) The final bit of dash was the diamond horseshoe stickpin, which he'd bought in 1916 at an auction for $92.50, and which he considered a good luck charm. He didn't have much hair, but what he had was slicked back, well oiled, and plastered down. It was his magnetism, not his looks, that presumably endeared him to his supporters (and also to the many women he liked to "visit" with as he traveled around the state). Some thought Bilbo's dandyism might get him into trouble with the state's poor white farmers, but it never seemed to hurt him. He even survived a charge by an opponent that he had been seen in public taking dancing lessons and eating caviar.

He was in many ways a progressive governor, in the peculiar fashion that Deep South politicians became progressives. Like his racist mentor James Vardaman, Bilbo combined his love of the white man (and hatred of the black) with efforts to help poor whites and stir up their resentment of rich people and corporations, the kind of resentment that had been a staple of political life in his home town. He fiddled with the tax codes to make corporations and utilities pay more and ordinary people pay less. He increased state aid to public schools. In later years, he called his program "books and bricks." Some people in the 1930s liked to compare him to Huey Long, and like Long he lashed out at "Wall Streeters" and rich corporations and the political old guard. Once he even told an audience that he thought "every man should be a king and every woman a queen," using Long's trademark phrases. But Bilbo was not nearly as skillful or smart as Long, and he was always getting into trouble. If it wasn't a scandal, it was one or another stupid decision that he stubbornly refused to change even though it was clear it would fail or hurt him politically, or both.

One of them involved the South African tick, a tiny insect he said was spreading Texas fever, a disease deadly to cattle. As governor, he pushed legislation requiring farmers to dip their cattle into chemical vats to kill any ticks they might be carrying. Farmers didn't like the idea. They feared the dip would kill their cattle along with the ticks. But Bilbo persisted, even after someone sneaked into the state's dipping yards and dynamited the vats.

By law, Bilbo couldn't run for reelection. Lee M. Russell, who succeeded him, hadn't been in the State House long when he became involved in a lawsuit. The complainant summoned Bilbo as the main witness, but Bilbo avoided testifying against his friend Russell by hiding in a barn. The case was dismissed for lack of evidence. But Judge Edwin R. Holmes gave Bilbo thirty days in jail for contempt. He served only ten, but even those days weren't wasted. His cell faced a street, and by shouting through the barred window he gathered a crowd outside. He told them about the injustice of his case and announced he would seek a second term as governor at the next election. He did, but the farmers remembered those livestock dipping vats and were still resentful. So he lost.

In 1927 his luck was better and he was elected governor again. This term was an unhappy one both for Bilbo and the people of Mississippi. His enemies controlled the legislature. He refused to sign its tax bills, and it refused to pass his. When his term ended, the state's treasury balance stood at $1,326.17, and appropriated obligations were $7,486,760.20. The state of Mississippi was broke. So was Bilbo—out of a job and out of money.

He began looking at the U.S. Senate. Senator Hubert D. Stephens, then representing Mississippi, fell ill during Bilbo's second term as governor. Hearing Bilbo was interested, he charged him with "waiting like a ghoul for me to die" so he could appoint a successor.

"Senator Stephens," Bilbo retorted, "is a vicious, malicious, pusillanimous, cold-blooded, premeditated, plain, ordinary liar." Later he added, "I was really very considerate of him. He was a sick man." But he didn't die in time for Bilbo to replace him. Bilbo was never a man to forget a grudge.

When he left the governorship, Bilbo campaigned for U.S. Senator Pat Harrison, then up for re-election in Mississippi. Harrison won and rewarded Bilbo with a $6,000-a-year Department of Agriculture job as a "consultant on public relations." What Bilbo really did was supervise a corps of women who clipped mentions of the New Deal's Agricultural Assistance Administration from newspapers and magazines. He denied that he ever dipped a brush into a paste pot, and he resented the name applied to him both in Mississippi and Washington: "the Pastemaster General." For a year he fussed with the AAA's scrapbooks and managed to see that his name appeared in its clippings occasionally, and that it was always properly spelled.

But Bilbo was not cut out to be an agency bureaucrat, and in 1934 he appeared suddenly in Senator Harrison's office and announced that he planned to oppose Stephens in the next race. Harrison told him to go ahead, but added, "I'll have to support Stephens."

"By all means do so," Bilbo said. "That'll give me my best campaign argument."

"What's that?"

"I'm going to say you now have two Senate seats in your pocket, but the Constitution calls for two men and I'm running for the vacancy."

Bilbo ran, and he put on the loudest, gaudiest campaign Mississippi had ever seen. He toured the state from end to end in his flivver. He threw barbecue parties for more than 18,000 persons. He sang "Bringing In the Sheaves," "The Ninety and Nine," and "Clementine," accompanying himself on the melodeon. He promised voters everything he could think of. He blasted such fanciful enemies as "farmer murderers, corrupters of Southern womanhood, and skunks who steal Gideon Bibles from hotel rooms." He said the state was ridden with Communism and needed him to cleanse it. (Forty-seven Communist votes were cast in the state that year.) He reminded the voters that Bilbo is a two-edged sword. "That's me," he said. "I fight coming and going." Most Mississippi newspapers hated Bilbo and tried to stop him, but he enjoyed their dislike of him and just campaigned harder. He once admitted that he liked campaigning better than holding office.

To attend a Bilbo rally was like being in the presence of a furious, tireless human windmill. He called for "a planned redistribution of the wealth," old-age pensions, and any other legislation he could think of, however unlikely it was ever to pass, to tax the rich and give jobs and cash to the poor. Then you might hear him give his famous description of himself: "Bilbo—what a man! A man of titanic energy, dynamic driving force, a wonder in sustained power of endurance, and a marvel of intellectual brilliance! The Man— Bilbo!"

In all, Bilbo made more than a thousand speeches, rising at 4 a.m. every day and traveling until after sundown. He not only won the election with 101,702 votes to Stephens's 94,587 but gained ten pounds in the process, mostly because he lived on a diet of sardines, cheese, and crackers. When someone asked him, "What's the population of Mississippi?" he answered: "Votin' or eatin'?"

Bilbo arrived in Washington in 1935 in the same dusty campaign flivver he had driven over Mississippi from Yellow Rabbit to

Vinegar Bend. He brought with him a blustery promise to "raise more hell than Huey Long," whom he had always disliked (partly because Long was very popular in Mississippi). There was some hope, and fear, that he and the Kingfish would tangle on the floor of the Senate, but Bilbo was too wary of Long's influence to battle him openly. They sniped at each other once in a while, but they never really fought. Bilbo sometimes called the Louisianan "the Crawfish" and said, "He better stay out of Mississippi." Long, who never minced a word, called Bilbo "just a plain damned fool." Bilbo shed no tears when Long was assassinated in 1935.

Except for the car and the hollow promises to take on Huey Long, Bilbo made almost no impact at all on the Senate in his first months. He took his seat and said nothing, following the tradition that a newcomer should be seen often and heard seldom. Finally he broke silence with a short speech admitting that "the real reason I ran for election was to get a place in the Senate garage to park my car." The outstanding event of Bilbo's first year was the grand opening of his briefly famous "Dream House" back in Poplarville, a twenty-seven-room monument to himself with five bathrooms, including his own, which was decorated in orchid and black. He invited hundreds of friends and served them a hundred pounds of cheese, ten cases of crackers, six hundred cans of sardines, five gallons of dill pickles, fifty gallons of ice cream, ten cakes, and eight hundred five-cent cigars.

Bilbo's first real, Mississippi-style speech in the Senate came when his colleague, Senator Harrison, nominated Judge Edwin R. Holmes for the Fifth Circuit Court of Appeals. Bilbo, remembering the ten days he had spent in jail at Holmes's order, took the floor and attacked him for five solid hours. The Senate listened patiently and politely, then confirmed the nomination. No one but Bilbo voted against him. That speech started a four-year feud between Bilbo and Harrison. When the Democrats elected a Senate leader in 1937, Harrison and Alben Barkley were the leading candidates. Barkley won by one vote—in Harrison's view, the one Bilbo cast for Barkley rather than for his fellow Mississippian.

Otherwise, Bilbo's Senate career was distinguished by its unabashed racism, which even in an all-white Congress filled with segregationists was notable for its viciousness. He realized after a while that as a member of the Senate he could introduce any piece of legislation he liked, however ludicrous and embarrassing, and then speak on its behalf for as long as he wanted. The other senators would have to sit in their seats, squirming, and listen to him. He could also speak against any measure he didn't like, as he did with the Holmes nomination. He launched two famous filibusters—one against a proposal to repeal state poll taxes (a device particularly popular in the South because black voters usually couldn't afford to pay them) and another against the 1938 bill to make lynching a federal crime (a bill motivated by the correct belief of anti-lynching activists that lynchers would never be convicted in local courts in the South). When issues involving race came up, Bilbo forgot about first-term reticence and jumped into the battle in full cry. In those debates, Bilbo usually found a way to introduce his pet scheme for solving the race question no matter what the actual topic was: his long-standing proposal to ship the country's black citizens to a colony in West Africa. During the poll tax debate, Senator William Langer of North Dakota asked him if he was still for "the bill he had here before, to send all the Negroes to Liberia"?

Bilbo was delighted to reply. "I introduced a bill to provide the ways and means by which they could be voluntarily settled in West Africa." It was, he insisted, a sensible way to create a "permanent solution of the race question which we have had before us, which we are having now and of which we will have more in the future."

Langer asked him how those sent to Africa would be selected.

"It is not a question of selection. That is merely a question of defining what a nigra is. A nigra is anyone who is ascended from the African race." One drop of African blood would be enough.

Other members of the Senate left the floor, or tried to pretend they were not hearing what they were hearing.

At other times, he supported his demand for the expatriation of black Americans by telling the NAACP the colored race could never expect fair treatment in this country and would be happier in a nation of its own. He said he was "the best friend the Negro has got" and claimed more than 3,500,000 blacks had endorsed his plan. Black leaders regarded it as ridiculous.

After speaking for three hours, Bilbo returned to the subject at hand, the poll tax, and offered a final piece of wisdom on the bill to outlaw it: "By the way, the idea of the pending piece of legislation came from Russia. Those behind it saw this as the opening way to make a stab at the very heart of the Constitution of the United States." The bill died on the floor.

Every senator is given a seat on some committee or other, and Bilbo—one of the least respected members—was put on the one considered least consequential: the District of Columbia Committee. There, it was thought, he could do no harm. But no one had counted on the effects of seniority, particularly in a committee that most senators left as soon as they could. In 1943, Bilbo became chairman of the District Committee, a job carrying the unofficial title "Mayor of Washington," since the city then had no elected government of its own and depended on Congress for its budget. It would have been hard to imagine a more alarming choice for the job of "mayor" of what was being called the "capital of the free world," because there was no one more likely to reveal to the world Washington's most shameful secrets.

Most white Washingtonians rarely saw black people, except when they had black servants in their homes or black service workers at their offices. But nearly a third of the city was black, one of the highest percentages of any city outside the former Confederacy, and the number was rising.

Every day, more black migrants streamed across the Fourteenth Street Bridge from Virginia: young men alone, with their possessions tied up in bundles carried on sticks on their shoulders; families, with small children in tow, sometimes bringing a few farm animals with them; refugees escaping the poverty of the tobacco lands of rural Virginia and North Carolina or the cotton communities of the Deep South. They were hoping for something better than long days in the field for low pay and large debts, but in Washington they seldom found it.

Few of the newcomers had access to the jealously guarded world of the black middle class ensconced on one side of Capitol Hill and in parts of Georgetown. So they did what generations of newly arrived African Americans had done before them. They moved to "the alleys," rows of tiny, shabby dwellings crammed behind row houses in the residential areas next to Capitol Hill. For a while after the Civil War, new Irish immigrants competed with freed slaves for space in the alleys. But after a time, the Irish moved on. The African Americans remained.

They lived in a squalor that some whites might have found more alarming had it not all been so conveniently out of sight. Alley dwellings often had no plumbing.

One water faucet on a pipe rising up from the ground was used by several houses. Open-ended barrels set down over holes in the ground served as privies—the city health department counted fifteen thousand of them—and were used by as many as thirty people each. The alley shacks themselves were crumbling, unpainted, unheated, and filthy.

Wherever they lived—on "the Hill" or in the alleys or in the crumbling Georgetown houses that were now being snatched up by New Dealers and converted into expensive housing—they looked out on a city that was rigidly and thoroughly segregated. Throughout the city, hotels, restaurants, movie theaters, libraries, and taxicabs refused to serve blacks. Retail stores, even those in black neighborhoods dealing with black customers, refused to hire black sales clerks. Dress shops allowed black women to buy clothes but wouldn't let them try them on. White residential neighborhoods were governed by strict covenants forbidding homeowners to sell their houses to blacks (or, in many neighborhoods, to Jews).

For years, the federal government had hired virtually no blacks—a few dozen janitors and messengers, but not many others. And while things had gotten a little better under the New Deal—blacks occupied enough significant offices that they were able to form an informal "black cabinet" to try to advance their goals—most of the federal bureaucracy remained under the control of whites from Central High School and the like.

This was the city Bilbo encountered when he became its unofficial "mayor," the place he promised to turn into "the model city of the world." He would not, he said, let the Washington establishment continue its passive, genteel ways. He would, he promised, shake things up. Washington soon learned that Bilbo wasn't joking. Every move he made was somehow related to his hatred of the city's black population and his efforts to subordinate them, or to send them away. In less than a month, the newspapers and church and civic organizations were crying for his scalp. The uproar started when the "mayor" of the nation's eleventh largest city made the following pronouncements:

• All the 20,000 persons living in the capital's alley dwellings, 90 percent of them African Americans, must move out within one year, thus clearing up the city's worst slums in one grand swoop. This ill-housed, low-income group had to find homes elsewhere—on their own. Those who couldn't had to go back to the farm, wherever that might have been.

• Washingtonians, barred by law from voting, should not be granted suffrage, according to Bilbo, even though they had been asking for it continually since Congress took it away in 1878. "If suffrage should be granted," he said, "the Negroes would soon have control of the city and the alleys would be outvoting the avenues." Much of his language on the subject of Washington's black population was a great deal more shocking than that.

The *Washington Post* immediately labeled Bilbo's new administration "An Adventure in Bigotry" and asked for his removal. The Southeast Council of Churches, calling him "anti-Christian and unpatriotic," asked for another District Committee chairman. The *Negro Tribune* called him "the Bilbonic plague," the National Association for the Advancement of Colored People said he was "unfit to preside," and the *Washington Daily News* said, "Throw him out." Hostesses in white Washington society made Bilbo a pariah, a crude and embarrassing figure never to be admitted into a respectable home.

Undeterred, Bilbo demanded a stiffer penal code for Washington, a city that at the time was almost completely free of organized or big-scale crime, and advocated taking back from the state of Virginia a thirty-square-mile strip of land that had once been a part of the District. The land had been given back to Virginia in 1846. "That," said Bilbo, reviving an issue a century dead, "was a mistake."

Washington was accustomed by sad experience to being governed by out-of-towners who knew nothing of its local problems. Residents had no voice in their own government. For decades, an act of Congress was required to change the hours for turning on streetlights or the days when shad could be sold in fish markets. Most residents had to some degree accepted their votelessness and political invalidism as a price they paid for front-row seats at the drama that is the national government. But in 1943, some of them began to think that Bilbo was setting the price too high.

What really started the organized campaign against him was a speech Bilbo made before the Mississippi legislature after his first month as District Committee chairman. It shocked most of Washington, official and otherwise, white and black. His remark that blacks "would soon have control of the city" if suffrage were granted in the District of Columbia was the starting point. He was horrified that some white and black government employees used the same cafeterias. He complained about white and black soldiers patronizing the same canteens, and wound up his tirade with a demand to "ostracize all who cross the color line." That kind of language might not have been unusual in Mississippi, or even in Washington, a decade or two earlier. But in the 1940s, with the nation at war, government officials were under pressure to behave themselves before the world. Bilbo ignored the pressure.

His Senate colleagues, reluctant to enter into the tangle Bilbo had woven around himself, said little about his Mississippi speech beyond that it was "unfortunate." Elsewhere the reaction was less restrained. Demands for his removal from the District Committee chairmanship were loud. Bilbo refused to resign.

Campaigning for re-election in 1946, Bilbo said that "the way to keep the nigger from the polls is to see him the night before." But ironically, the most unvarnished racist in the Congress was under attack from his opponents in Mississippi that year for being—of all things—soft on white supremacy. Earlier in his career, Bilbo had campaigned against the poll tax in Mississippi—not because he had wanted blacks to vote, but because he knew that the tax also kept from the polls many of his poor white supporters in the hill country. Now his opponents used this against him. With the war over and black soldiers returning determined to claim the rights they had been told they had been fighting for, white supremacists everywhere were ratcheting up their rhetoric. Bilbo had to struggle to keep up. "In this fight for white supremacy in the South," his opponents said, "we must have men in Washington who believe in the poll tax." Never mind that Bilbo had filibustered against poll-tax repeal. Never mind that he had called for U.S. blacks to emigrate to West Africa. Never mind that he had once recommended making Eleanor Roosevelt "First Lady of Liberia."

Bilbo won the election despite their efforts, but he lost his "mayoralty" in the process. Republicans now controlled the Senate, and the chairmanship of the District Committee went to one of them. Bilbo had other worries by that point: stopping the now very serious effort to bar him from the Senate. Glen Taylor, a liberal Democrat from Idaho, called for the Senate to investigate his colleague's behavior because it "reflects seriously on the in-

tegrity of this body." Republicans expressed horror at Bilbo's call for barring
blacks from voting in Mississippi in 1946.
"Never to the knowledge of the under-
signed," a group of Republican senators
said in a committee report, "has such vile,
contemptible, inflammatory, and dangerous language been uttered in a campaign
for the purpose of procuring nomination
and election by an incumbent and member
of the United States Senate, sworn to up-
hold the Constitution." Those senators had
obviously not spent much time in the
South.

Once the new Congress convened, other
senators began investigating Bilbo's relations with war contractors. There were
charges, probably true, that he had used his
Senate position to win war contracts for
friends and had received generous payoffs
in return. It seemed almost certain that the
Senate would vote to deny him his seat.
But Bilbo was now nearing seventy, and
while he was still able to raise a ruckus, he
was sick. In the middle of the battle to un-
seat him, he suddenly disappeared from
Washington. A few days later, word came
that he was back in Poplarville, dying. The
campaign to bar him from the Senate fiz-
zled. And a few months later Bilbo was indeed dead.

For years after, Bilbo (and "Bilboism") became a symbol for a kind of unvarnished, unreconstructed racism that most white people in Washington liked to think was beneath them. The city was, of course, still segregated. Black families continued to live in alley dwellings. Nothing very much had changed. But now that they had "gotten rid of" Bilbo, it was possible for white Washingtonians to return to their comfortable, genteel ways, unreminded of the racial problems around them. Herman Talmadge came to the Senate in the mid-1950s as a senator from Georgia, after serving as governor and proving himself just as determined a segregationist and white supremacist as Bilbo, but Washington hostesses lionized him because he was so polite and courteous and "refined," because he wasn't anything like that crude, terrible, foulmouthed man from Mississippi who wasn't fit to enter their drawing rooms. Bilbo had become, in the memories of white Washingtonians and of most members of Congress, something like a bad hurricane—an awful event that had blown through town, shaken things up, and then was gone, leaving the city free to settle back into its old ways, its old habits, its old prejudices, for just a little while longer.

Martin Dies

Before there was Joe McCarthy, there was Martin Dies, a big-boned, cigar-smoking Democratic member of Congress from Texas who was the architect in 1938 of the original House Un-American Activities Committee, which he chaired for seven consecutive years. It was known as HUAC, informally pronounced "hughack." And in Dies's days of high-flying extremism and hell-raising, it was pronounced often in Washington and throughout the country. He was one of the first of the fervent and tireless Communist hunters, and one of the first scalps he might have hung on his wall—had he been lucky or energetic enough to find any evidence against him—was Alger Hiss, whom he fingered as a Communist long before Whittaker Chambers did, but he could not make the charges stick until Richard Nixon came along and took up the case in 1947. When

I moved to Washington in the early 1940s, he was already famous as the leading anti-communist in Congress—to some people a hero, to most of us in the press corps a buffoon. Over the next ten years, we watched him expand his charges, until he finally exhausted his credibility and left the field to others.

He was a Democrat, but for years he bucked the New Deal. And when Congress—at the instigation of New York Congressman Samuel Dickstein, who was furious at the sight of brown-shirted American Nazis marching through the streets of Manhattan—set up HUAC to investigate fascist subversion, Dies prevailed upon his fellow Texan, Vice President John Nance Garner (by then another Roosevelt hater), to hand the committee over to him. Dickstein and others might have wanted HUAC to investigate fascists, but Dies knew from the start that he would go after Communists, which he claimed included most members of the New Deal. He wreaked havoc in sundry corners, helping to shut down the Works Progress Administration and the Federal Theatre Project, and forcing the president of the University of Texas to resign. He investigated Hollywood, the labor unions, and people committed to civil rights, a cause he disparaged as "utterly senseless." In less than two years, using his committee's swollen budget, Dies and his feverish investigator, J. B. Matthews—a reformed Kentucky Communist—gathered enough information about private citizens to fill 145 filing cabinets which, they said, the FBI consulted daily. Among many others, he named as Communist sympathizers Bette Davis and Shirley Temple, the child actress. Harold Ickes, the secretary of the interior, ruminated that "now the great committee has invaded the nursery and next it will be seizing her dolls as evidence."

Dies dealt in large round numbers, saying seven million "subversive elements" were running loose in the United States, 50,000 Communists served in the U.S. armed forces, another 50,000 controlled the CIO, and 100,000 more held white-collar jobs in sensitive war-related industries—their names he reportedly kept on index cards. Another 165,000 Americans—most of them naturalized citizens—carried Communist Party credentials in their pockets, according to Dies. All this, he said, in addition to two million "fellow travelers" camouflaged by a "Trojan horse" of consumer, pacifist, and youth organizations. Dies had a special fondness for denouncing the two thousand "garden variety crackpots" in the Roosevelt administration, including Interior Secretary Ickes, Labor Secretary Frances Perkins, WPA director Harry Hopkins, and the First Lady, Eleanor Roosevelt. "These people had a mission on earth," he proclaimed, to make America a Kremlin satellite. In a controversial, unpublished HUAC report, Dies once called FDR "the Kerensky who precedes the dictator."

Needless to say, Martin Dies Jr. rubbed the Roosevelt administration the wrong way. The president often restrained his cabinet and top advisors from responding to Dies's insults, but in the fall of 1938, Roosevelt lost his cool. HUAC had been up and running for just a few months, and Dies had assured the public that he would not allow character assassinations or "any smearing" of innocent people. "The Chair wishes to make it plain," he said, "that this committee is not after anyone." But on this particular October day, Dies accused Michigan's governor Frank Murphy, an ardent New Dealer, of demonstrating a "treasonable attitude" when he refused to call out the National Guard in 1937 against sit-down strikers in the automobile industry. After excoriating the strike action as "an open challenge to law and order," Dies wondered aloud whether Governor Murphy, a future Supreme Court justice, was a Communist or merely a Communist dupe. Reporters rushed to FDR, clamoring for a response. With steely gentility, the president said that his impromptu remarks might not be printable. He issued a written statement some hours later, charging that Dies had attempted to influence Murphy's re-election with tactics that were "flagrantly unfair and un-American," and added that "any response from me would not be printable." He praised the governor's level head and diplomacy, which, he said, had avoided bloodshed. "For that act a few petty politicians accuse him of treason; for that act, every peace-loving American should praise him."

Dies, delighted and flattered that the president had even taken notice of him, went on the radio and vowed to be David against Goliath. "I shall do my duty, undeterred and unafraid," he promised.

Dies was born in 1901 in the piney woods of East Texas. No one knows much about his early years, but people in Texas said he grew up helping his mother run a dairy farm. The Dieses were not what southerners called "quality folk"; their lineage, re-

ported *The Nation,* could not be traced beyond the congressman's father, Martin Sr.,
a Louisianan transplanted to East Texas.
Dies Sr. earned a law degree and was, at
different times, a newspaper editor, county
judge, and district attorney. He practiced
law in Orange, Texas, and in 1908 won a
seat in Congress in the second district,
which his son would also represent. It was
an impoverished region of cut-over timber
and sandy cotton fields along the Louisiana
border. In 1939, a writer described the
Dieses' constituents this way:

> As proud as they are poor, the hill
> people represent an almost undiluted
> Anglo-Saxon stock, many of whose
> forefathers were among the early set-
> tlers of Texas. Deeply religious, re-
> served, suspicious of any newcomer,
> they bitterly resent the small foreign
> strain brought into the district by the oil
> wells. For the most part they work in
> the sawmills—when they are run-
> ning—or scrabble for a living in the un-
> fertile soil. Families are large and
> clannish, and feuds are common.

The district had 70,000 black residents,
all of them barred from voting. Dies Sr.
was known as a xenophobic isolationist,

always angry at the South's oppression by the high tariff, the frightening influx of radical immigrants, and what he saw as the vulgar transformation of suffragists into "manly women." He asked Congress to affirm its commitment to "the white man's domination of this Government." And like many white southerners, Dies Sr. hated labor unions. "Let this be a free republic," he shouted, "secure in property rights and secure in individual rights where, in the name of God, the blighting shadow of Bolsheviki socialism may never come to haunt our dreams!" He also hated Woodrow Wilson's internationalism. "You know," he once said to great applause on the House floor, "as God shall judge me when I stand before him—and I believe He lives—the best hope of this great Government, the best hope of this great people, and the children yet to be born from the loins of men and the wombs of women, is to live in this hemisphere and attend to our own business." He vehemently opposed the League of Nations, pleading that America not be ruined by "insidious foreign advisors." Wilson retaliated by campaigning against Dies's re-election, to no avail.

Years later, in 1930, when he was twenty-nine, Dies Jr. won his deceased father's seat and along with it a little fame for a moment by being the youngest member of the House. But he was best known on Capitol Hill for being the lanky young man who liked to sprawl on government-issue couches in the House cloakroom, smoking nickel cigars, and offering a stream of wisecracks and imitations of his colleagues' speech patterns. Among his other triumphs, he invented the Congressional Demagogues Club, committed self-mockingly to "flamboyant speeches saturated with hokum." At one of his first congressional picnics, Dies took FDR by the arm and bellowed, "Ladies and gentlemen, let me introduce the Demagogue-in-Chief!" With that foreboding exception, there was little to suggest that his would be a notable career.

Otherwise, Dies roused himself mostly to vote for every spending bill and against every tax increase, and to introduce bill after bill his father would have loved, including one to expel, restrict, or deport "all alien Communists, dope peddlers, gangsters, racketeers, criminals and other undesirables." He blamed immigration for the mass unemployment of the Depression. And he complained bitterly of Roosevelt's "army of paid parasites," who were, he said, coming as trespassers into the South and bringing with them all sorts of unwelcome nostrums, promoting nutrition, pushing unionism, and opposing the poll tax, lynching, and white supremacy. He once expressed his outrage when a group of southern sharecroppers wrote a letter to Congress complaining of the bleakness of their lives: "Why were these people not complaining about poverty in the northern slums." Convinced that the sharecroppers were being encouraged by Eleanor Roosevelt, he accused her of "outrageous lies."

Dies was fortunate in having a friend in House Speaker Garner, a fellow Texan who became Roosevelt's first vice president. Garner got him a seat on the powerful Rules Committee, the springboard from which Dies later took over HUAC—but not until he had spent years complaining about the New Deal's "fruitless experimentation" and its "ever-increasing desire to have the Federal government act as wet-nurse for every local community and state in these United States." He also began to see fighting Communism as an attractive line of work, and he got his start by, among other things, denouncing the WPA's Federal Theatre Project. When someone in an appropriations hearing mentioned in passing the playwright Christopher Marlowe, who died in 1593,

Dies asked, "This Marlowe. Is he a Communist?"

In 1938 he was enthroned as HUAC chair. In his committee hearings, photographers were given the run of the room. Spectators and witnesses exchanged taunts, and committee members shouted insults at each other. Audiences were encouraged to stand up and cheer pronouncements by the chairman. The Capitol police once had to stop one member, Representative Joe Starnes—a hard-line reactionary from Alabama—from physically assaulting a witness. But Dies never allowed radio broadcasts of his hearings, saying he did not want anyone "acting the monkey for public entertainment."

From his seat on HUAC, Dies announced that he had unearthed an elaborate Soviet plan to indoctrinate black Americans. "Moscow realizes," he said, "that it can never revolutionize the United States unless the Negro can be won over to the Communist cause." He went on, "I deplore the fact that throughout the South today subversive elements are attempting to convince the Negro that he should be placed on social equality with the white people, that now is the time for him to assert his rights."

HUAC was the most reviled committee on Capitol Hill among New Dealers and others. But every year the House voted overwhelmingly for its reauthorization and in 1945 made it a standing committee. It was a committee dominated from the beginning by southerners uneasy with the New Deal. And Dies never missed a chance to attack it—even after Roosevelt's death, when he said, "Everybody who knew the inside story knew perfectly well that whenever you mentioned the name 'Russia,' Roosevelt would come to life. And of course, Mrs. Roosevelt was more so than the President." On another occasion, he accused Roosevelt publicly of having planned the Japanese attack on Pearl Harbor and blamed him personally for the deaths of "three boys who used to play on my front porch." (This "information" came, he said, from published sources at the Library of Congress.) He claimed that Mrs. Roosevelt pressured him to exonerate her confidant, Joe Lash, who Dies said was a perjured Communist, so he could secure a commission in naval intelligence. The vice president (then Henry Wallace) said that "Dies could not harm America's morale any more if he were employed by Hitler." The Federal Communications Commission reported that Dies received more favorable and frequent mention on German radio during the war than any other American. Father Charles Coughlin, the anti-Semitic radio priest, named Dies his "Man of the Year" in the same year that Coughlin began denouncing "Jewish Communists" in his radio broadcasts. No witness called to testify before the Dies committee—unless he was there to identify and denounce Communists—was treated without contempt and savagery. Every witness was greeted with the same question: "Are you now or have you ever been a member of the Communist Party." When one responded, "I will answer your question in full if you will allow me a few words of explanation," another committee member, J. Parnell Thomas of New Jersey, shouted back: "You may explain nothing! Answer the question!"

And yet despite it all, the voters in Texas and the people surveyed in public opinion polls continued to trust and support Dies; and other members of Congress were, as they would be later, during the McCarthy era, too timid and fearful to vote against him or his committee. And so HUAC survived, even though its original mission—looking for fascists in America—was almost entirely ignored and, after 1945, made irrelevant.

If there was one man in America who could give Dies a run for his money, it was Walter Winchell, the powerful gossip columnist who had his own formidable reputation as a hater of fascism and communism and who was famously vindictive. Winchell grew up dirt-poor on the Lower East Side of Manhattan, the son of Russian Jews. He loved Franklin Roosevelt and detested anti-Semites.

Winchell and Dies had been close once. After HUAC was founded, Winchell funneled information to Dies about American fascists, but the two had a falling-out when Winchell began to accuse him of being soft on fascists. In the early spring of 1944, Martin Dies demanded that NBC Radio give him equal time to the attacks, and he threatened to subpoena Winchell and his scripts to prove that "fully 60%" of his statements were "un-American propaganda." A deal was struck allowing Dies to speak for fifteen minutes on the March 28 broadcast, with Winchell to follow with his response. At nine o'clock on the appointed evening, Dies took the microphone at WMAL, a Washington NBC affiliate. He informed his audience that he had come, not to trade insults with Winchell, but "to fix the attention of the American people on one of the most sinis-

ter forces this nation has ever faced." Dies
defended HUAC's investigative record,
claiming that "hundreds of pages of docu-
ments" had been supplied to the Justice
Department to help prosecute domestic
fascists. Winchell's real motive, he said,
was to destroy Dies and others like him
who opposed making the president "an
all-powerful central executive." Winchell,
he said, was a "transmission belt to deliver political propaganda, handing it on,
sandwiched in between his collection of
divorces, infidelities and other social dere-
lictions." Dies closed with his signature
prophecy, telling his listeners that "to preserve our freedom," America must win
two wars, the one in Europe and the ideological war at home.

Winchell—the professional radio man—
repeated his charge that Dies pampered
Nazis. "Far from retracting a single statement, I reiterate every one of them," he
said bluntly. The public sided with
Winchell.

Within the month, Dies announced that
he was stricken with cancer of the larynx
and would retire, which got him out of the
limelight just as the limelight was becoming unpleasant. But he had no cancer, and
in 1952, with his brand of anticommunism
in fashion again, Dies was back in Con-

gress, having won both the Democratic and Republican nominations for an at-large congressional seat. "This gives me a chance," he told his constituents, "to help finish the job of housecleaning that I helped to start in 1938." But by then, the House had changed, and Dies never got another seat on HUAC. Even the Republican conservatives, who welcomed investigations into Communism that they thought might embarrass the Democrats, saw Dies now as too crude and irresponsible to entrust with the job. In 1956, he lost a special election for the Senate, and retired from politics two years later. He died of a heart attack in 1972—having become a tiresome irrelevance and faded away.

J. Edgar Hoover

The most enduring, and also the strangest, figure of my years in Washington was J. Edgar Hoover. I barely knew the man myself, but from the time I arrived in 1943 to Hoover's death in 1971, he was always a big figure in the lives of those of us who were following the government.

I knew about Hoover long before I came to Washington, because he was already, in the 1930s, one of the most famous men in America—and a man who attracted the particular interest of young boys. He was, I grew up believing, a crime-fighting hero, storming into buildings with his men to arrest dangerous criminals. There were magazines and comic books and radio shows that celebrated his exploits, and every boy I knew took at least some interest in him. When I got to Washington as a young man in the forties, Hoover was still a larger-than-life figure—not quite so central to popular culture as he had once been, since so much attention had shifted to the war, but still a huge figure, lionized in Washington just as he was by all the young boys reading about him in true crime magazines. He was leading the effort to root out fascists. He was busting people who violated wartime laws—mobsters, profiteers, even traitors. Washington and America seemed to most people to be safer places because Hoover was around.

After the war, Hoover had a rougher time. That was ironic, actually, because the great passion of his life was fighting Communism. The first big event of his career was organizing the Palmer Raids in 1919—the notorious roundup of suspected radicals ordered by Attorney General A. Mitchell Palmer. Hoover had to scramble to distance himself from the raids once they were revealed as the sham they were. He didn't let them destroy his career the way they destroyed Palmer's. But he never lost his hatred of Communism and his conviction that rooting it out of America was one of his, and the FBI's, most important jobs. So the fifties should have been a great time for Hoover, with fear of Communism running at high tide. And in some ways it was. It gave him license to divert substantial Bureau resources to investigating Communism, and it made it possible for Hoover to associate himself with one of the great issues of the day. But the anticommunist world of the 1950s was a crowded place, and Hoover had a hard time seizing the credit he wanted. He also had to guard himself against the excesses of some of his fellow warriors. Although it was the FBI that built most of the case against Alger Hiss, Hoover let Nixon take the principal credit for it because he was afraid the effort would backfire. And he realized earlier than most that Joe McCarthy was a dangerous loose cannon and never let himself get drawn into his orbit. McCarthy had to conduct his shabby investigations using his own incompetent staff. The FBI would have little to do with him.

Gradually, I began to realize that Hoover was not the bold, heroic crime fighter so many people believed him to be. And he wasn't really the demonic, power-crazed figure that his critics started to think he was in the 1960s. Or at least he wasn't just those things. He was, at heart, one of the most familiar Washington characters, one of the people that all of us realized were the lasting centers of power in the federal government: he was a quintessential bureaucrat. The directorship of the FBI wasn't a civil service job. But with Hoover there, it might as well have been.

There have always been two Washingtons, living in uneasy proximity to each other. One is the Washington of the politicians—the presidents and members of Congress and the political appointees to the agencies and the many other people who flow in and out of the city with each election cycle. The other is the permanent Washington, the city's lifers, people whose lives change little no matter who is in the White House or on Capitol Hill. That includes the merchants and the doctors and the local lawyers; the taxi drivers and janitors and cleaning women; the bankers and insurance salesmen and real estate brokers. It also includes the lifetime bureaucrats, for whom the federal government is as much a local business as steel plants are in Pittsburgh and coal mines are in West Virginia. Generation after generation of mostly white, mostly middle-class Washington kids grew up attending local public schools, going to Georgetown or Catholic University if they were Catholic and George Washington if they weren't, maybe getting a law degree from one of the local universities, and then spending their lives working in secure civil service jobs in the federal government.

Hoover was, at least in spirit, one of them. He had grown up in a white middle-class neighborhood on Capitol Hill. His father and his grandfather had both been government bureaucrats, and Hoover never thought of doing anything else. He went to George Washington Law School, got a job in the Justice Department, rose up in the ranks, and never left. It was only his fame and his power that differentiated him from the thousands of other lifetime government workers.

Hoover's personality was almost a caricature of the cautious bureaucrat. He now has a reputation as someone who used his power recklessly and irresponsibly, and maybe he did at times— but not, I think, knowingly. He was at heart a person obsessed with order and routine. Never married, he lived with his mother in the family's house on Capitol Hill until he was thirty-eight, when she died. Then he moved into another house in northwest Washington, where he lived until he died himself. Nothing in his home ever changed. He numbered the signed photographs hanging on his walls so that they could be hung in exactly the same place when the rooms were painted every few years (always in the same colors as before). He ate lunch at the same table at the same restaurant every day. He took his vacations in the same place in the same weeks with the same people every year. His companion through his whole adult life was his deputy Clyde Tolson, and while their relationship may or may not have been sexual, it was certainly something like a marriage—as stable and comfortable and, it seemed, devoid of passion as many conventional middle-class marriages.

What really made Hoover the perfect bureaucrat, though, was his instinct for preserving his position. Like civil servants who know they will outlast their bosses of the moment and refuse to commit to anything they think might jeopardize their positions when the next boss comes in, Hoover ingratiated himself with one president after another but resisted doing what they wanted him to do unless he thought it would serve his own interests. Given his excesses in other areas, some people were surprised to learn that he had scuttled the Nixon administration's "Huston plan" for using the FBI and other agencies against Nixon's political enemies. But Hoover's opposition had nothing to do with principle. He thought the plan, if it was ever made public, would jeopardize his job.

Hoover got into trouble, finally, when his usual instincts failed him—in the sixties, when many people found that their lifelong habits and assumptions suddenly didn't work anymore. He went after Martin Luther King Jr. and the civil rights movement and the student left and other liberals and radicals because he believed that the rest of the political world, and the public, was, like him, horrified by all these challenges to tradition. But this time, he was out of sync with his time, unwilling or unable to figure out that the culture was changing and that his instinctive defense of the white middle-class world he had grown up in was not what the public world was interested in. He survived, but not without damage. In the late 1960s, for the first time in his career, a president, Nixon, tried to shoehorn him out of his palatial office in the Justice Department (an office, by the way, bigger and grander than that of the president or the attorney general). Hoover fought him off, but his reputation was already unraveling when he died in 1971.

He lay in state for a few days in the Rotunda of the Capitol. Almost no one came to see him.

May Craig

Twice each week, reporters gathered in the White House pressroom to await Franklin Roosevelt's briefings—one held in the mornings for the afternoon newspapers and one in the afternoon for the following morning's papers. We idled around in a lobby outside the president's office and piled our hats, coats, and cameras on a hideous round table—a gift from a former president of the Philippines, lavishly carved to look like some kind of aquatic animal.

Steve Early, Roosevelt's press secretary, sometimes offered us quiet suggestions about what questions might produce newsworthy answers. He worried that when the president had something interesting or important to say, no one would ask the appropriate question. We almost always waited a few minutes—time for Roosevelt to make sure he had enough cigarettes to get through a half hour with reporters. Because he smoked, we all thought we could do the same. But we never did. Holding a notepad and pencil and a cigarette while standing on the president's carpet with no ashtrays was too awkward. So we all stood while the president sat behind his desk. He almost always began by saying he had "no news today" but would answer questions. Whatever the questions, however, he usually found a way to turn the conversation to things he was thinking about—and more often than not, what he was thinking about was the press. He seemed continually furious about what the right-wing papers—the Hearst and Patterson and McCormick papers, whose publishers despised him—were saying about him. He called newspaper columnists "excrescences." At which point a sharp female voice usually came out of the crowd standing around his desk and said something like "But, Mr. President, you've got a newspaper columnist in your own family." (Eleanor Roosevelt wrote a widely distributed column called "My Day.") The question came from Elisabeth May Craig, a reporter for the Booth newspapers in Maine and one of the few women correspondents in Washington— usually the only woman at the briefings in the president's office. She looked a little like Helen Hayes, small and prim with a softly lined face, blue eyes, and curled hair fastened with whalebone. She wore signature pink pearls and one of thirty-two different pink floribunda hats. She got her start in the 1920s. Her husband Donald, then Washington bureau chief for the *New York Herald,* wrote a column on the side for the *Press Herald* in Portland, Maine. When he was injured in a car accident, May pitched in and wrote the column for him. Not too long after that, Guy Gannett hired her as Washington correspondent for his chain of Maine newspapers; and for more than forty years, she wrote daily dispatches and a weekly column called "Inside Washington." "The column is really me," she said. "I don't have time to polish it, and I know that it's ungrammatical at times. But I think it's awfully good, myself."

Around Washington, folks used to call her the most famous journalist never read, since her audience numbered fewer than 100,000. But she almost always managed to make herself heard, with her "dodge-proof" questions and her sharp tongue. She was quick to criticize politicians she considered evasive. She liked to say that Franklin Roosevelt possessed a "delightful discursive way of avoiding questions." Of Harry Truman, she said, "He answers the first question so quickly that he is on to the next one before we've found the loophole in the first." She was frequently annoyed at Henry Stimson, Roosevelt's secretary of war, because he opened his briefings by saying "Good morning, gentlemen!" while staring right at her. She even had the nerve to criticize Truman's decision to add a balcony to the south front of the White House. The building, she believed, was not his to alter.

May was something of an actress, and her best performances were always at press conferences—what she called the "grass roots" of the news business. The sight of this wrenlike woman sitting in the front row, sparring with presidents and high government officials, was entertainment in itself. May spared no one, not even Eleanor Roosevelt, her close friend. On national television in the 1950s she broke ranks with her fellow reporters and asked Mrs. Roosevelt, who was wearing a pink hat she had borrowed from May, about reports of her son's marital infidelities.

She was a scrappy feminist long before modern feminism came along. In 1947, when she was the only female reporter accompanying Truman to Rio de Janeiro, she gave him a tongue-lashing when she was forced to return home by plane, and not with the rest of the press corps aboard the battleship *Missouri*. The navy said it had no facilities for women on the ship. As the first woman elected to the Standing Committee of Correspondents of the congressional press galleries in 1945, she promptly ordered that a women's restroom be built, complete with horsehair sofa.

The war decade was her finest time. Although she wrote for a modest audience, she covered the invasion of Normandy, the V-bomb raids in London, the liberation of Paris, the occupation of Germany, and the creation of Israel. In the end, she received a theater ribbon from the war department. She was the first woman reporter to fly in the Berlin airlift, the first to cover the Korean truce talks, the first to fly over the North Pole. In 1944, she started broadcasting for Maine radio, which led to a slot as an interviewer on the radio show *Meet the Press.* When the show moved to television in 1947, May moved with it and asked the questions she thought ordinary Americans wanted answered. Television turned her into a minor celebrity, known far beyond her readership in Maine.

Although her flinty style made her seem like a native New Englander, she was actually from the South. She was born in 1891 in the South Carolina low country, and she grew up on Coosaw Island, a remote little place near Beaufort. But she left South Carolina while still a girl, when her mother died and her father sent her to live with relatives in Washington. She liked writing, but had no luck with fiction. She thought about becoming a nurse, but married and raised two children instead. She always found time for causes, though. She marched in a suffrage parade during Woodrow Wilson's inauguration, and she organized one of Washington's first PTA chapters. Her husband's accident in 1923 and his death ten years later pushed her life onto a different course.

Starting out as a journalist, she knew that being a woman—and a small one at that— would be a handicap. She discarded her southern drawl and shortened her byline. She also "decided a number of things *not* to do. I think women's voices are too high, and I think they smile too much trying to be pleasing, and I hated their laughter, even on radio. I made up my mind I'd rather be grim than giggly." People sometimes called her "granite-faced" or "sharp as cider vinegar," and cartoonists and comedians lampooned her. Her very feminine wardrobe—and particularly the trademark hats, which she never appeared in public without—seemed almost incongruous against her tart, aggressive style.

She liked things in order. She served the same chicken recipe at every dinner party, because she knew how it would turn out. A colleague once asked her how she managed to keep the same white dress wrinkle-free day after day during a Washington heat wave. She told him she had been wearing four different dresses, one each day. If she liked a dress, she bought the same one over and over. "I plan everything I do," she said. Craig remained a very visible character into the 1960s, and in fact some of her most memorable moments came when she tangled with President Kennedy during his televised press conferences. After Kennedy's death, though, she became more pessimistic, even a little crabby, and criticized what she thought was a wrong turn in American life. "Unless there is a change, deep down, in the American people," she warned in 1964, "a genuine crusade against self-indulgence, immorality public and private, then we are witnesses to the decline and fall of the American Republic." She denounced the sexual revolution and predicted it would lead young people to ruin. She didn't much like the new feminism of the late

1960s either. But that was at the end. She had lived much of her life by a feminist creed, and more than that, she had lived as someone who loved adventure and thought what she did was the most exciting work anyone could do.

Frances Parkinson Keyes captured May's essence when she wrote, "There is an elemental simplicity and wholesomeness about her such as one associates with fresh-baked bread, russet apples, sweet clover and other pleasant things like that."

May died in a Maryland nursing home in 1975.

Joe McCarthy

No one roiled the world of Washington in my time more completely than Joe McCarthy, an unimpressive junior senator from Wisconsin who got elected in 1946 by lying about his war record and slandering his opponent. Once in the Senate, he spent three years not knowing what to do and therefore doing virtually nothing, until early in 1950 he realized he would have to run for re-election soon. And since being in the Senate beat any of the other jobs he had tried and failed at in the past, he looked hard for an issue he could use to remain in office.

The story goes that he thought about the St. Lawrence Seaway and other public works ideas that might interest people in Wisconsin, until one night at dinner in the Colony Restaurant a few cronies told him that Communism was the new hot thing and that he should try it. It wasn't quite as simple as that, because McCarthy had already discovered the joys of anticommunism when he smeared his opponent, the distinguished Robert La Follette Jr., as one in 1946. He hadn't used the issue for a while, but by 1950 he was impressed by how well attacking Communism was working for others—Richard Nixon, Parnell Thomas, Pat McCarran. And so he decided to give it a try again, beginning with his now-famous speech in Wheeling, West Virginia, in 1950 when he claimed to "hold in my hand" a list of Communists in government—and found, probably to his amazement, that he was soon one of the most revered, reviled, and remarked upon figures in America.

I barely knew McCarthy myself, but I did have a connection with him. My sister Mary, who as a divorced young woman with a child moved to Washington to look for a job, started working in the early 1950s in McCarthy's office as his executive secretary, privy to all his activities. Like most people who knew McCarthy by reputation, I hated the man. But she adored him. And through her accounts of him, I learned a little about the other side of McCarthy—sappy, sentimental, warmhearted, and most of all, perhaps, drunk. That was a good description of several of my sister's husbands, and so maybe it wasn't all that surprising that she liked her boss. But she liked him most of all because he was nice to her, which her husbands usually weren't, and she developed an extraordinary loyalty to him—so much so that years later, when McCarthy's career ran off the tracks and he became the subject of government investigations, Mary testified about him before a senate committee and (according to Bobby Kennedy, who worked on the committee staff and told me this many years later) lied for him on the stand.

McCarthy was in many ways someone who never grew up, and he brought all the destructiveness of his reckless youth into adulthood, where it was infinitely more damaging—to other people, and in the end to him too—than it had been back in Appleton. But there was also something almost, but not quite, charming about the man, in the way he seemed puzzled that people he publicly attacked and destroyed did not respond to his friendly gestures once the cameras were turned off. To him, it was all an act, and he half expected his victims to go along with the joke and join him for a drink when the show was over. But for them, of course, it was not an act. It was a life-changing trauma. McCarthy

never quite understood why so many people hated him, why men who had once
been his friends began refusing to shake his
hand or turned their backs on him when
he came near. That didn't stop him,
though, because the benefits of his crusade
seemed too enormous to trade for friend-
ships.

He did keep some friends through it all:
some of his own staffers, whom he treated
like drinking buddies, and others who
worked in the Senate Office Building,
who liked to come by his office at the end
of the day. There McCarthy took a pair of
dice out of his desk drawer, and he and the
staffers and other visitors and hangers-on
had a crap game on his carpet. The stakes
were one-dollar bills, and a fifth of
whiskey was passed around hand to hand
while the dice were rolling. A time or two,
at the end of the day, his crap game over,
his cronies gone, and the bottle empty,
McCarthy could be found asleep in his
government-issue leather chair, snoring.

McCarthy came to Washington a roguish
bachelor. He eventually married a member
of his staff and tried to settle down. But it
was too late for him by then, because the
booze had taken hold, and he could not re-
strain himself—either in politics or in his
personal life. He careened ahead, getting

more and more reckless with his accusations and his lifestyle, taking on enemies that were in the end too much for him: Eisenhower, George Marshall, CBS, *Time,* and eventually the U.S. Army. His undoing, finally, was the famous Army-McCarthy hearings, set up by Eisenhower and some of the Senate Democrats to bring McCarthy down—and so they did. The most celebrated exchange of the many days of these hearings, which were—almost for the first time, since the medium was so new—televised live, was McCarthy's joust with the Boston lawyer Joseph Welch, who reacted with fury when McCarthy attacked one of Welch's young associates for having Communist associations. "Have you no decency, sir, at long last?" he asked him as if incredulous at McCarthy's recklessness. It turned out that Welch had known the attack was coming and had carefully rehearsed the whole performance. It wasn't Welch alone who brought McCarthy down. Lots of people contributed to that, not least McCarthy himself. But Welch was as good a symbol as any of the decency that McCarthy never understood and never adequately feared.

A few years later, repudiated by the public, censured by his colleagues in the Senate, far gone in his alcoholism, McCarthy died, pathetically, from the effects of years of uncontrolled drinking. He never thought of himself as a bad man, and he seemed always to believe that if he was friendly to people in private, he could be forgiven what he did in public. He would have been surprised, I suspect, by the depth of the hatred he inspired among otherwise generous people, and by the reaction to his death—which I've always associated with my first wife, who was driving the kids home from school one day when she heard the news on the radio that McCarthy had died and said, to their great puzzlement, "Good!"

Everett Dirksen

Everett McKinley Dirksen—a man with a portentous name incongruously shortened to Ev—was an immensely likable gent who really wanted to be a Shakespearean actor, but who found few employment opportunities consistent with his ambition in his home town—Pekin, Illinois. It was too limited for his talents, and so he reached beyond it, finding happiness in the United States Senate, where a more welcoming stage awaited him. There he could rise at any time and speak to the other members, and under Senate rules he could talk as long as he liked on any subject he liked. The other members did not necessarily stay in their seats to listen when Dirksen rose to speak, since no one ever knew what he would talk about.

When he chose, he spoke at great length about the virtues of the marigold—a flower according to some, a weed accord-

ing to others—which year after year he insisted should be made the official flower of
the United States. (As far as I know, the
country has never had an official flower.)
"See the pretty marigold," he said in a
voice that rumbled with the baritone notes
of a Wurlitzer organ, "nodding its sweet
yellow flower in the cool evening breeze,
turning itself into the globular roundness
of late summer, offering itself to the winds
to carry its little cobweb of seeds to the
world, to the suburban lawns, to the roadside and farmlands of our precious America and to the yards of widows and
orphans, an act of holy generosity no one
here today can match." On other occasions, he would praise the beauties of the
rose, as if working his way through the
Burpee seed catalogue.

In his first years in Congress, Dirksen
was known mostly as a sharp-tongued partisan. But by the late 1950s, he had become
a character—a beloved, if at times exasper-
ating, figure who attracted tributes that
were almost as fulsome as his own oratory.
For example, *Time* magazine—which has
its own reputation for fulsome prose—
once compared Dirksen's oratory to the
tinkling of the crystals in the Capitol chandeliers: "But hark! Whence comes this
counterpoint that shivers the crystals into

new and shimmering song? It comes from the man behind the desk—a big-handed man with a lined cornfield face and graying locks that spiral above him like a halo run amok. . . . He fills his lungs and blows word-rings like smoke. . . . 'Motherhood,' he whispers, and grown men weep. 'The flag,' he bugles, and everybody salutes. Whew! No one who has seen this performance will ever forget it."

Dirksen was born in 1896 to German immigrants in Tazewell County, Illinois, not far from Peoria, and given the middle name McKinley for the newly elected Republican president. (His older brother had been named for the previous Republican president, Benjamin Harrison.) Central Illinois was Republican country, and Dirksen's parents were devout partisans. They were also strict Calvinists. Dirksen's father died when he was young, but his stern mother reared the boys alone. Like most of their neighbors, they worked a small piece of farmland, raising their own food and selling the surplus. It was Everett's job to peddle fresh milk each morning before going to school. So he got up well before dawn to give himself time to read before his chores. When he wasn't working or reading, young Everett liked to make speeches. "There was a certain ruggedness about life," Dirksen said of his early years. He described them sometimes in the words of Lincoln, who had also lived in central Illinois, as "the short and simple annals of the poor."

He worked hard and was a good student, and when he graduated from high school his classmates diagnosed him with a malady they called "Big Worditis." He became the first member of his family to go to college, entered law school, and then dropped out to join the army when America entered World War I. That was in part to protect his family from the anti-German hostility that was sweeping much of the country. When he got back to Illinois after the war, he tried his hand at the washing machine business and with a dredging company before settling in with his brothers to run a bakery. But he was always restless. He wrote short stories, novels, and plays (few of them ever published) and acted in a local theater company, where he met Louella Carver, whom he married in 1927. He thought about going to Hollywood, but he made a promise to his dying mother, whose Calvinist soul rebelled at the idea of her boy living among the sinners of the film world, and turned instead to Washington, which his mother somehow considered a more upright place.

In his first race for Congress in 1930, he lost by just 1,100 votes to an opponent who called him "the baker boy from Pekin." Dirksen said afterward, "It was true. For a livelihood, I worked at the dough bench with other bakers in our shop, making cookies and rolls and bread, or engaged in driving a truck, delivering toothsome doughnuts, coffee cakes, and bread to retail stores. A menial and altogether plebeian occupation." He started campaigning for Congress again almost immediately, and two years later he won a narrow victory in a district that Franklin Roosevelt carried—the first Democrat to win it in years. In Washington, he finished his law degree at night and rose to prominence as a grandiloquent critic of the New Deal. He had gotten elected originally on an isolationist platform but, in 1941, he supported the president's decision to lead the country into war.

In 1949, he gave up his seat because he had been diagnosed with a serious eye disease that doctors said might blind him, and even kill him, without surgery to remove his right eye. But at the last minute, Dirksen decided not to have the operation, saying that a bout of prayer had convinced him he didn't need it. He and his wife moved out to a house they kept on the

Chesapeake Bay, where he tended his flower garden. Gradually his vision improved, and a year later he was back in Illinois, running for the Senate against his friend Scott Lucas, then the majority leader. He won in a landslide, capitalizing on Truman's unpopularity and his own staunch anticommunism. Once in the Senate, he was one of Joe McCarthy's strongest defenders, and when his colleagues decided McCarthy had become intolerable and resolved to censure him, Dirksen refused to go along on grounds, he said, of "Christian charity and brotherly love."

But Dirksen never paid the price for partisanship that other politicians did, partly because everyone found him so likable. "If we have to have Republicans in Congress," Sam Rayburn once said, "let them all be like Senator Dirksen." He was endearingly disheveled, his suits always rumpled and never quite fitting properly, his wavy hair sticking out in all directions. "His face looks like he slept in it," one reporter said. As he grew older, Dirksen developed severe bags under his eyes, so he wore a pair of weighty black glasses with no lenses, to hide them.

He never lost his taste for theater. When he became Republican leader in 1959, he started a weekly news conference with his

House counterpart, Charles Halleck, that the press liked to call the "Ev and Charlie Show." He liked to sit on a table, blowing smoke rings as he entertained questions. He became more and more fond of his own rhetorical flourishes, and nicknames started to spring up: the "Wizard of Ooze," the "Liberace of the Senate," "Irksome Dirksen." Bob Hope once described his voice as a cross between Tallulah Bankhead and Wallace Beery. In 1967, Dirksen won a Grammy for a documentary album he recorded, titled *Gallant Men,* that included "The Star-Spangled Banner," the Pledge of Allegiance, and the Gettysburg Address. It went gold, selling more than 500,000 copies, and he made two other albums soon after. He appeared often on television, not just on *Meet the Press,* but also with Red Skelton and Johnny Carson. In 1968, he led the Rose Bowl Parade in Pasadena, casting doubt on his loyalty to the marigold. At the end of the year, he and his family hosted their own Christmas special on national television.

During his decade as minority leader, from 1959 to 1969, Dirksen became not just a character, but a statesman. When disgruntled Republicans complained that Dirksen was too soft on the Democrats, he would say, "We are not going to oppose just to be opposing." In the realm of international affairs, he nearly always supported the president, believing as he did that "we cannot as a minority show a disunited spirit to the world." Without Dirksen's help, Kennedy probably could not have gotten his nuclear test-ban treaty ratified in 1963. Dirksen was critical to Johnson's success in winning passage of the Civil Rights Act of 1964, lining up enough Republican votes to break the southern filibuster. Some critics pointed to Dirksen's frequent changes of mind on issues. He responded, "The only people who don't change their minds are in cemeteries." At the 1968 Republican National Convention, Dirksen stood at the podium, greeted by thunderous applause, and barked into the microphone, "Quiet!" When the crowd finally calmed, he leaned forward and said solemnly, "I accept the nomination."

Dirksen was from an area of Illinois often called "Beantown," after a favorite local crop. And he was as fierce a defender of the bean as he was of the marigold. At one point, when he discovered that the Senate dining room had no bean soup on its menu, he introduced a resolution on the floor—which his colleagues approved—requiring "that the humble little bean should always be honored." Bean soup remains on the Senate dining room menu still, every day. "There is much to say for the succulent little bean," Dirksen said. "Not only is it high in nutriment, but in that particular kind of nutritious value referred to as protein, the stuff that imparts energy and drive to the bean eater and particularly the Senators who need this sustaining force when they prepare for a long speech on the Senate floor. I venture the belief that marathon speakers of the Senate going back as far as the day of the celebrated 'Kingfish,' Senator Huey Pierce Long of Louisiana, and coming down to the modern marathoners in the forensic art such as Senator Strom Thurmond of South Carolina and Senator Wayne Morse of Oregon, both of whom have spoken well in excess of 20 hours and felt no ill effects, would agree the little bean had much to do with this sustained torrent of oratory."

Dirksen's heroes were Abraham Lincoln and William Jennings Bryan, midwestern champions of the common people. In his last years, before his death in 1969, he complained often about the way America was moving away from its traditions and its religious faith. But he never got too discouraged. He could always find solace in the pages of the garden seed catalogue.

Jimmy Hoffa

At the center of Washington, D.C., with
a clear view of the United States Capitol,
stands a white marble edifice so elegant it
looks like a particularly lavish government
building. It is the national headquarters of
the International Brotherhood of Teamsters. It was built by the union's one time
president Dave Beck. He ordered it
sheathed in white marble despite the hor-
rific cost, and when queried about this he
responded: "It never needs painting, and
do you know how much union painters
are paid these days?"

Beck was later indicted, convicted, and
driven from the presidency, his place taken
by James R. Hoffa, known to everyone
as Jimmy—who became legendary as the
toughest, most unyielding union leader in
the country. He was a rough and ready
man, usually wearing the white socks and
plain clothes of a working stiff. He had

spent years building up the Teamster local
in Detroit into one of the most powerful,
and, many believed, most corrupt, in
America. In the late fifties, he moved into
Beck's marble palace and ran the union
from there for almost a decade, until he
too was convicted and jailed and eventually murdered.

The Teamsters Union is still in the news
sometimes, for many of the same reasons it
used to be. Ron Carey, a "reform" president elected in the 1990s, was removed
from office and indicted for campaign finance scandals in his own campaign. He
was succeeded by James P. Hoffa, who appealed to members remembering the gravy
days of his father's leadership. But Carey
and the younger Hoffa are at best pale imitations of the snarling, brawling, tough-as-
nails Jimmy. In the 1950s and 1960s, he
was one of the most famous men in the
United States, and one of the most reviled.
Many people hated him just because he
was an aggressive union leader with a no-
holds-barred style of battling employers.
But most people thought of him as a gang-
ster and saw in him and in the Teamsters a
dark and dangerous force that threatened
the nation. I myself contributed to this image, saying at one point that "the Teamsters Union may be the second greatest

power in this country—second only to the
Federal Government. It certainly is our
biggest, richest union. It's in every state
and directly or indirectly in every industry.
And its members have been accused of, indicted for, or convicted of maybe half the
crimes known to the law. It is a profound
force in American life."

Fear of Hoffa and the Teamsters probably
reached its peak in 1962 and 1963, when
Bobby Kennedy made "getting" Hoffa one
of his main goals as attorney general. And
in April 1963, with a union election soon
to occur and after many requests, Hoffa
agreed to do an interview with me for
NBC. I don't know why he decided to talk
with me after having refused requests from
many other people on television. We had
never met, he considered me a "jerk," and
when we first started filming him—he was
speaking to a union meeting in Detroit—
he pointed to our camera crew and said he
was going on my program "knowing quite
well what I'm letting myself in for . . . I assume in a very derogatory way." But whatever other people thought of Hoffa, he
thought of himself as a leader, a man of the
people. And I believe he probably agreed
to let me put him on the air because he
thought if people saw him as he was, they
would think better of him. He said to the

crowd we were filming, "No matter what they may say, the people of this country will know one thing—we don't have to hide for what we do; our actions speak for themselves." Hoffa did have a lot to hide, and he knew it. But I feel he really believed what he said—that the core of what he did as a union leader was despised not because it was wrong, but because people feared what he could do for his members.

For my part, I wanted to interview Hoffa partly just because he was a big story, but also because I wanted to try to understand how this man—under criminal investigation for most of his career and running for re-election as head of his local in Detroit while standing trial for fraud—was so popular with his truckers.

The union election in Detroit in 1963, which we were there to observe, had all the apparatus of a democratic election: secret ballots, two outside observers (a lawyer and a priest). Every union member had his identity checked and had to sign for his ballot. As far as we could see, it was an honest election. It was also unique because it was the first time in Hoffa's career that anyone had bothered to run against him. His opponent was a truck driver named Ira Cooke who said he ran because Hoffa was on trial and because two other union officers had already been convicted of taking payoffs but were nevertheless running for office unopposed. He didn't have a chance. Most Teamsters jeered that Cooke had been handpicked by Bobby Kennedy. Hoffa won with 95 percent of the vote.

Hoffa had powerful allies in locals around the country. Anthony Provenzano was the president of a big Teamster local, the third largest in the country, in Hoboken, New Jersey, and vice president of the international. He was known as "Tony Pro," and when he held rallies, he saw to it that they were rallies not just for himself, but also for Hoffa and for solidarity in the face of the enemy—the enemy being not only employers, but critics, the law, and, most of all, Bobby Kennedy. In early 1963, Provenzano was under two federal indictments, one for extortion and one for taking payoffs from a trucking firm. He was not as popular as Hoffa and won his own race for re-election with only 55 percent of the vote. But however shaky his popularity might have been, he knew Hoffa's was not, and he did everything he could to associate himself with the great man and with the cause that Hoffa himself so often described—raising up the workingman by fighting the rich and powerful. Provenzano warned his members of "a vast and damning conspiracy directed against Teamsters everywhere," a conspiracy hatched by "corporation kings and the princes of industry, protecting their vast expense accounts and salaries and luxurious yachts." Of course, the conspiracy also included Bobby Kennedy, "because of his personal vendetta against not only James Hoffa . . . but myself and also the entire Teamster movement, which includes yourselves. They must know that our two million Teamster members overwhelmingly support us . . . If we are called too powerful because we have tried with all our souls to serve you; to lift you from your toils and make you secure, then we plead guilty."

In Philadelphia, a union officer named John Backus tried to explain Hoffa to us. He attributed his popularity to his "attention to so-called bread and butter issues— that is the pay envelope, giving a reasonable amount of money to everybody so that the average Teamster can go out and buy the things he feels are necessary for his family's well-being." But Hoffa was also popular, he said, because of Bobby Kennedy's "vendetta" against him. Another union official chimed in, "Jimmy Hoffa has not only been a benefactor to the people that are affiliated with our international union, but has been a benefactor to all of the people in the labor movement in the United States and he has done that . . . knowing that almost every group of people that are anti-union have attempted to put every obstacle that they can think of in his path. And with all of those obstacles, he stood tight and he fought for the people who worked and that to me is an honest, sincere, courageous labor leader."

Hoffa's popularity was visible every time he came within sight of his members. They usually wouldn't talk much with us, but they talked with him—shouting encouragement as he walked through union halls or when he stood on the stage; speaking to him like one of the guys. "Mr. Hoffa, I thought Samson was a giant. But you're a labor giant!" "Hey, Jimmy—when you get through with that hat give it to me. I can use it." "Bobby Kennedy won't win this election, don't worry about it. We're going to win it." "You're the man. You make us stand up and take notice."

Obviously one important source of Hoffa's power was that he saw to it that his members got the money. But another reason for his hold on their affections was precisely what made him so hated by others: that he was a tough guy, that he stood up to the heavyweights, that he had powerful enemies who could never quite get him. When asked about corruption, Teamsters either dismissed it as a smokescreen created by the Justice Department or dismissed it as unimportant because Hoffa delivered the goods.

There was opposition. In Philadelphia, we talked to the leader of a group called the Voice of the Teamsters, a remote ancestor of the better-known dissident group, Teamsters for a Democratic Union, that began in the 1970s, after Hoffa had been deposed. In November 1962, they almost won an election, and they were working hard toward defeating Hoffa's ally, Ray Cohen, in the next one. Cohen dismissed them as "misleaders" and said he wouldn't "belittle myself to meet with such individuals." The Voice leader did plenty of belittling on his own. He once suggested that there was a connection between being short and being a tyrant. Hitler, Stalin, Castro, and Khrushchev were all five-foot-five, he said, and so were Hoffa and Cohen. One Voice ally described Hoffa as "a parasite . . . a blood sucker, tryin' to suck the blood from the honest truck drivers of the nation . . . an egomaniac." But people in the Voice campaigned against Hoffa at their peril. Another Voice supporter tried driving around Philadelphia with a sound truck denouncing Hoffa and Cohen. He came back to report that he had been followed by five or six carloads of Hoffa men, who pinned him in between a tractor-trailer and their own cars, pulled him out from behind the wheel, and kicked him in the face. "They're crazy, those lunatics," he said.

But Hoffa didn't really need thugs to keep the members in line. He had them in the palm of his hand, and the more he talked about the forces trying to get him, the more passionate they became in their support for him. "We are facing a struggle as never before," he told his local in Detroit in 1963. If his opponents got their way, the result would be "the kind of unions you have in Russia. . . . And I promise you, despite the propaganda that will be heaped upon us in the next three years of office, that I am ready at any time to appear in front of this membership and answer for any single thing I do and you be the judge."

My interview with him took place in his splendid office overlooking the U.S. Capitol. Beck, who designed the place, was devoted to the flashy and expensive, and the office had suited him. Hoffa seemed out of place there, with his cheap clothes and his unshined shoes and his general lack of interest in material surroundings. He still lived in the same modest house in Detroit he had bought in 1939 for $6,800. He claimed to give much of his salary to charity—although he admitted that one reason he did so was because it helped him politically. The office was pretty much as Beck had left it, and Hoffa used it without seeming really to occupy it. He worked long hours, was always willing to see any union member, hated to write letters, loved to talk on the phone—and loved to talk generally, especially about himself. With me, he took on the manner of an ordinary man, "an average human being," who had become the target of extraordinary enemies, a guise he often assumed and one that he presented with alternating layers of anger, defiance, and self-pity.

I started out by reading something the columnist Max Lerner had recently written about him, saying that Hoffa saw life as a jungle and the law as a trap to be got out of. Hoffa didn't deny it. "Of course life is a jungle," he said. "Anybody who thinks that it isn't just isn't around. . . . Every day of the average individual is a matter of survival. If by chance he should go from home to work and have an accident, lose an arm or leg or an eye, he's just like an animal wounded in the jungle. He's out. Life isn't easy . . . and if you're not careful and fully aware of it you're in trouble."

When I asked him about ethics, he didn't hesitate for a moment. "What may be ethical to you may be unethical to someone else. I'm not unaware that a lot of people disagree probably with my actions, my ethics. But my ethics are very simple. Live and let live and those who try to destroy you, make it your business to see that they don't and that they have problems."

By the time I talked with him, he had been president of the international for six years and had lived in Washington much of that time. He still hated the place. "I think there's more con men in Washington than there ever was in a carnival," he told me. "There isn't a single thing I find in Washington that is real. It's a make-believe fantasy." He talked about members of Congress saying one thing in a closed committee room and a completely different thing in public. Hoffa disliked that. "A lot of people don't like what I say but I say what I think and if I tell you something I won't tell three other people something different."

He had no doubts that Bobby Kennedy was waging a personal vendetta against him. "The record speaks for itself," he said. "He has 32 grand juries in the United

States looking to the affairs of the Teamsters Union." Why was Kennedy doing this? "In my opinion, he has never in his life run up against a situation he couldn't dominate. . . . He's just a spoiled young millionaire that never had to go out and find a way to live by his own efforts, and he cannot understand resistance to what he wants." What Kennedy wanted was a union movement that wouldn't stand up to the president or to big employers, but "we don't intend to conform. We're going to carry out what our membership wants . . . whether Robert Kennedy likes it or not."

Hoffa didn't think much better of the press than he did of the Justice Department. "There isn't a single newspaper in this country that I know of . . . that won't follow the national press releases without question, and whatever comes over the wire service will appear in their paper even though it's a repeated lie." But he claimed to take comfort from polls he'd commissioned that showed that the American people were behind him. "You can't convince the people in this country that the FBI, the Justice Department, the policing agencies in their own towns are all in Hoffa's hip pocket."

Although Hoffa tried to sound like what he called an "ordinary man," his conversation was that of someone who knew how to hate. Along one wall of his palatial Washington office was a chest (with a stone panther sitting on top) filled with the printed hearings of the McClellan committee, whose antiracketeering investigations in the late 1950s had first brought Beck and Hoffa to the attention of federal law enforcement authorities. (Bobby Kennedy worked on McClellan's committee staff at the time.) The Landrum–Griffin Act of 1959, which McClellan helped push through Congress, was one result of those hearings—a law to make "gangsterism" and "racketeering" harder for unions to get away with. Of particular importance to the Teamsters, it made it more difficult for unions to use boycotts against companies doing business with firms the unions were striking or that were making deals with rival unions. That kind of boycott had been a staple of Teamster tactics for years.

Hoffa hated McClellan almost as much as he hated Kennedy, and he didn't even try to disguise the depths of his grudge. He called him a "faker. Flat, right out a faker." In his mind, McClellan was always playing to the crowd, finding ways to make Hoffa look bad by asking him specific questions about things from "fifteen, sixteen and twenty years" ago. "They trade on the fear, and they trade on the atmosphere they create by having 150 newspapermen sitting there, having ten–twelve cameras, tremendous lights trained at the witness. Having eight senators sitting there; a staff of a hundred and fifty investigators and pounding away with insinuations that there's something wrong with the fellow unless he's experienced, and has gone through it before and knows it's all a fake, he can't take the pressure." Hoffa was not the last person to make complaints like that about the circus atmosphere of investigations in Washington.

I came away from my conversations with Hoffa both strangely impressed and deeply repelled. He was a man who knew the value of force and violence in keeping control over his union, but it wasn't just through force that he maintained his power. He was a man capable of producing higher wages for his members, but that wasn't the key to his power either. Most union leaders do that.

So how did he keep the loyalty of his members? How did he survive his conflicts with the law and the enormous media censure he received day after day? In just the two years prior to my interview, fifty-two people in or associated with the Teamsters had been convicted—of stealing union money, taking payoffs, violence, tax evasion, and perjury. But in union politics, at least, Hoffa emerged from it all unscathed.

Hoffa told me he thought life was a jungle, and for many people—including many members of his own union—it was. In the jungle, everyone is out for himself, and the most people can hope for is to find someone smarter and stronger than they are to help them fight off their enemies. To those people, Hoffa was a leader who knew the jungle, who knew how to fight in it, and who knew who his friends were and, at least as important, who his (and their) enemies were. A leader can survive a great deal, at least for a time, if he has the ability and the shrewdness to exploit his problems and turn them into assets. Hoffa knew how to make use of the attacks leveled against him. He turned them into evidence of exactly the view of the world he thrived on, a view of the world his supporters shared. People were out to get him, he made them believe, because they were afraid of being gotten themselves. Morality had nothing to do with it. The law had nothing to do with it. It was self-interest against self-interest, and the toughest guy would win. And Hoffa was the toughest guy around— for a while.

Lyndon Johnson

I first knew Lyndon Johnson as a fervent New Dealer in a political climate in which the New Deal no longer counted for much. He was a young, ambitious congressman from Texas. Later I knew him as the Senate majority leader, probably the most determined and effective majority leader in modern history. I once heard this conversation between two members of the Senate:

"Why are we about to pass this bill? What's it about?"

"I don't know. Lyndon wants it."

That was all that needed to be said.

He was a master at browbeating, bullying, and cajoling the slim Democratic majority in the Senate into doing what he wanted, which was also, often, what President Eisenhower wanted. Johnson's talents included compromising with the White House and leaving the president believing that Johnson's ideas were his own.

Then, in 1961, he became vice president and seemed almost to shrivel up into invisibility. He recalled a famous statement by former vice president and fellow Texan John Nance Garner, who once said, "The Vice Presidency? It's not worth a pitcher of warm spit." The vice presidency was a terrible job in those years. Johnson was isolated, disliked and even ridiculed by many of the Kennedy people, and had almost nothing to do. He tried to keep up his usual frantic pace, and occasionally—as when he went on a foreign trip unsupervised by his White House handlers—he succeeded. But mostly he was miserable. He later described those years, privately, as almost a kind of death.

No one could have become president under more terrible circumstances than Johnson did, and yet he handled himself very well in his first days in office. He was genuinely shaken by the events he had witnessed in Dallas, and for a while he seemed—incredible as this may sound to say about the man—humble. I have always thought that his restraint and dignity at that critical time did a lot to reassure Americans, and the world, about the stability and continuity of the nation.

But it didn't take long for Johnson to take to his new job. Theodore Roosevelt, when he succeeded the assassinated William McKinley in the White House in 1901, said, "It is a terrible thing to become president under these circumstances. But it would be even more terrible to be morbid about it." Johnson was not morbid for a minute, although for a time he was quiet, an unfamiliar posture for him. But soon he was his old self again, full of plans and proposals, constantly talking and moving and persuading, trying to control everything and everyone.

Like most people in Washington, I had never expected Johnson to become president. He was, we thought, too southern, too country, too gawky and awkward to get elected. But I had never had many doubts about his ability. And in time he became the most impressive but also, in some ways, the most appalling of the eleven presidents I have known. Once in the White House, he seemed to run the office as if it had been his all along. His first year was an election year, and Johnson was almost obsessed not just with getting elected, but getting elected by a landslide. To do that, he had to prove to the party and the country that he was up to the job, that he could get things done. He pushed through Congress some major legislation, including the 1964 Civil Rights Act. That hurt him politically in some areas of the country, but the net result of his activity was to make him seem powerful and effective and in charge. Because he had the good luck to run in 1964 against Barry Goldwater, who appeared to go out of his way to allow his opponents to portray him as a half-crazy extremist—which he was not—Johnson won by one of the greatest landslides in American history.

By the time Johnson won his victory, he had already given some indication of what he wanted to do. Fifteen presidential task forces had by then set out to produce fifteen reports; the sum of their ideas would constitute what Johnson was already beginning to call a Great Society. None of the fifteen reports was surprising to him, since he had personally chosen all the task force members. The American political road was already littered with task force reports offering to cure this or that national ailment. Most of them had been read lightly and politely, if at all, and then tossed aside and forgotten like empty beer cans. But in this case, they got some action, not because the reports themselves were any better than those that preceded and followed them, but because they were placed in the eager hands of a president compulsively and restlessly driven to do something. Johnson was one of the most skillful, factory-trained political mechanics ever to occupy the White House. But he was also attracted to what he considered big ideas. And he seemed really to believe in a radical notion: that it is possible for the mass of mankind to be happy.

His simple faith was that happiness was not, as Jefferson saw it, a goal to be pursued and perhaps never captured, the joy mainly to be found in the chase. Johnson saw happiness instead as a possession to be acquired and worn like a new pair of warm socks. A perhaps oversimplified glimpse of his attitude could be seen during a campaign stop in Ohio in October 1964. A crowd had gathered in the street to hear him speak. Some Goldwater posters surfaced, and there were angry shouts and a little ruckus. Johnson put aside his prepared text, looked out from under his creased and mournful brow, and said, "Now don't pay any attention to all that. You folks come on and be happy."

In other words, Johnson saw the goals of his task forces and advisors and well-wishers not as abstract descriptions of the attractive but unattainable. He thought that happiness was not only attainable, but that it could be achieved primarily through economic means, that there was no reason why a prosperous society could not guarantee material well-being, and thus happiness, to everyone. Johnson also had the time, the means, and the mind to take those ideas seriously, as none of his postwar predecessors did.

Harry Truman's troubled times didn't allow him the luxury to be imaginative or experimental. He was faced with serious problems that were immediate, ugly, and already at the gates. He first had to find out what the atomic bomb was, since President Roosevelt had never told him about it, and then decide how to use it. The Russians were taking over Eastern Europe and, a little later, threatening Greece and Turkey. Western Europe was bankrupt. And while Truman fought one war in Korea, he had to fight another at home against Joe McCarthy, who was so terrorizing the Congress that its members were afraid to expose his lies for fear that he would politically destroy them. Truman's responses had to be tough, instinctive, and fast. With the world seemingly on the brink of annihilation or totalitarianism, he could not afford to be philosophical or utopian.

Dwight Eisenhower was even less creative. He had been educated by the army and knew little about civilian politics. His biggest problem was his secretary of the treasury, George Humphrey, an implacable conservative. The reports of Eisenhower's task forces all called for more money for failing schools, crumbling cities, and struggling farmers, but each of them was stopped dead by Humphrey because, he said, they were too expensive. Eisenhower could have overruled him, but he didn't have the conviction to do so.

John Kennedy was a skillful politician and was receptive to new ideas, but he was not a great legislative mechanic, and the response to him in Congress was slow or nonexistent. The members knew him as a junior senator who even as president still stood in awe of the congressional elders, with their layers of seniority and habits of command. They remembered that Kennedy had barely been elected at all. And there was the unstated problem that many members of Congress were country boys while Kennedy decidedly was not. A congressman from Tennessee told me in 1962, "All that Mozart string music and ballet dancing down there and all that fox hunting and London clothes. He's too elegant for me. I can't talk to him."

He could talk to Lyndon Johnson. In the spring of 1964, while trying to settle a railroad dispute, Johnson called a meeting of railroad presidents in the White House. The president of the Illinois Central rose with a question, saying, "Mr. President, I'm just a country boy . . ." Whereupon Johnson in a broad theatrical gesture placed both hands on his own left rear trouser pocket, gripping his wallet, and said, "Hold on, now. I've dealt with country boys before, and I'm holding on to my pocketbook. Now what was it you wanted to say?" Kennedy could never have done that. But Johnson got the railroaders to do at least some of what he wanted.

What Johnson lacked in academic training he made up for with cunning, energy, and a vast knowledge of the workings of Congress. He was the only president ever to come from the Senate leadership and so he was able to push through Congress much of Kennedy's legacy—the civil rights bill and a tax cut, helped along by the suggestion that these were Jack Kennedy's monuments, hard to vote against in the year after his death. But many of Johnson's legislative victories were the result of his own relentless politicking.

For example: Representative Otto Passman of Louisiana was a subcommittee chairman in charge of foreign aid. And he had devoted his legislative career and such talents as he had mainly to cutting the aid, always along with his off-key tromboning about how much money he had saved the taxpayers. Year after year, he had his way, usually cutting the requested appropriation by about 20 percent. ("The deal was to set the amount we needed and then pad it so Otto could cut it and be a hero," said a foreign aid administrator.) Johnson could have continued with this relatively innocuous bit of political theater. But early in his presidency, he decided he needed to show, in a decisive but not explosive way, that there was a new president who knew more about Congress than any man in it. After some careful thought, he chose foreign aid as the place he would make that assertion.

The White House had little fear of antagonizing Passman. He was so far to the right of the Democratic Party that there was little hope of keeping his support for long. And so Johnson privately set his new administration to work persuading members of Passman's subcommittee to vote against the chairman's cuts and approve the full amount, and he did so quietly. When the vote came, the committee ignored Passman and voted the requested amount, and he found himself outvoted and his modest little dukedom suddenly in shambles. He was enraged but helpless, and Washington's power center had been moved a few feet further from the Congress and closer to the White House.

The federal establishment then and now might largely be seen as a money-handling machine, a few of its motors and gears devoted to bringing the money in, even fewer devoted to counting it and storing it, and all the rest devoted to spending it. This last section of the machine is almost totally operated by congressmen, and that is where hammerings, wrenchings, and occasional squirts of oil can most effectively speed, slow, move, and change the policies of the government. And it was in precisely that part of the machine where Johnson had spent his formative years as a politician and had learned mechanical skills unmatched in Washington. Once he was president, it was where he most often devoted his energy. Johnson's work of persuasion was ceaseless. Everyone had stories of the "Johnson treatment," on the telephone or in person; of how the president persuaded, cajoled, flattered, threatened, intimidated, bribed, extorted until it was almost impossible to resist. He had a compulsive energy, an insatiable appetite for work. (He once telephoned a senator at 11:30 p.m. on Christmas Eve to talk about the budget.)

Johnson, in other words, was a president who was an activist and a politician, not a philosopher or a stylist. Kennedy had quoted Kant and Mill and other authorities (even if straight out of *Bartlett's Familiar Quotations*) and achieved a degree of intellectual authority as a result. Johnson never quoted anyone more obscure than Jefferson and the Bible. His real authority was his ability to get things done.

But Johnson was not, at heart, the pragmatist that Kennedy was. Kennedy is remembered today by many people as a great idealist, but while he inspired a lot of idealism in others, he was unromantically practical himself. Johnson is remembered as a wheeler-dealer, but in fact he, more than Kennedy, was attracted to "big ideas." He belonged to the tradition of American leaders who believed that the goal of government was to move the nation further toward perfection. His rapturous notions about ending poverty, curing disease, rebuilding cities, improving schools, and creating a society where no one needed to worry about what he called "the ancient enemies of mankind" were so pleasing to contemplate that they inspired dreams of something like utopia, a place of perfect equality and happiness, which we could attain if only the government could be induced to work hard enough at it and spend enough money.

In the 1930s, during the New Deal, some Americans inspired by Roosevelt and by the ceaseless activism of his administration began to believe seriously that something like a utopia could be created in America. (In Britain, the Labour Party was edging toward a similar vision; Labourites sometimes called it the "New Jerusalem.") Roosevelt himself never quite believed that, although some of his advisors probably did. But he did nothing to discourage people from thinking that this was the goal of the New Deal. Some of the experts and advisors around Roosevelt wanted a sort of welfare utopia that would make pain and poverty disappear. They took a few steps in that direction: Social Security, labor legislation, wages and hours laws. It was the first time the utopian idea ever had any official status in America, the first time the power of government was committed in any substantial way to eliminating the everyday pains and miseries of human life. Until then, it had largely been every man for himself.

Lyndon Johnson was educated by Franklin Roosevelt. His first real political job was running a New Deal National Youth Administration program in Texas. He was elected to Congress for the first time in 1937 by being the only candidate in the race to support Roosevelt and his policies fully and unreservedly, even the controversial Supreme Court–packing plan. As a congressman, he did everything he could to ingratiate himself, and identify himself, with the president. Roosevelt noticed and helped him when he could. When Roosevelt died, Johnson said, "He was just like a daddy to me."

After the war, with the New Deal less politically useful in Texas, Johnson began to take some conservative positions and to align himself with traditional southern Democrats. But his New Deal enthusiasms remained powerful, if hidden, and they burst into view almost as soon as he became president. It was his goal, he sometimes said, to be the greatest domestic president in American history, even greater than Roosevelt. He would bring the New Deal at its most utopian back to life, and take it further even than Roosevelt had envisioned. But it was not to be.

One of the major projects of Johnson's "Great Society" was to fix every one of the terrible problems of the American city—its slums, crime, welfare rolls, race riots, crowding, dirty air and dirty water, deteriorating schools, rising taxes, and increasing ugliness. Large amounts of money and energy were devoted to eradicating all these social ills, and some useful things were done. But the idea that all this could be accomplished by the government was based on the familiar American fantasy that some called the illusion of bureaucratic omnipotence: the illusion that government can do everything, and should. That if every bureaucrat had enough ideas and energy and enough money to spend, everything wrong in the cities— and everywhere else—could be fixed and cured. Watching the Johnson administration pursue this illusion recalled a short poem by Samuel Johnson:

How small of all that human hearts endure,
That part which laws or kings can cause or cure!
Still to ourselves, in every place consigned,
Our own felicity we make, or find.

The tremendous enthusiasm with which the Congress, and much of the public, greeted the Great Society when Johnson first started trying to build it did not last for very long. The War on Poverty, in particular, became unpopular quickly. That was partly because of the problems and inefficiencies that resulted from the Community Action Program, which tried to give citizens control over programs that affected them. This was a favorite goal of some of the people around Robert Kennedy, and some of the leftover Kennedyites in the Johnson administration. Johnson supported it, probably thinking it would be a good way to make himself popular with local elected officials; and in some cities, that's what it did. But Community Action also produced class conflict and confrontation, something Johnson had not wanted. It got a lot of bad press, and it helped sour the country on the whole idea of a war on poverty.

But the real reason that the War on Poverty lost its popularity is because deep down inside most Americans is an admiration for those who have overcome difficulties and risen to achievement by their own efforts. Our folk heroes fit that pattern: Andrew Jackson, Abraham Lincoln, Thomas Edison, Jackie Robinson. Lyndon Johnson himself was more a self-made man than all but a handful of our presidents. For better or worse, this has always been a country that admires self-made men.

By then, I was a television newsman on NBC, and Johnson became quite attentive. He showered my wife and me with presents and phone calls and flattering notes. He gave one of my sons a summer job in the White House. He invited us occasionally to informal dinners at the White House, to formal occasions, to weekends at the LBJ Ranch and Camp David. Johnson's obsessive attention, flattering as it was, could also be oafish and bullying, as I later discovered.

Despite the public's misgivings about the Great Society and despite his personal shortcomings, Johnson might have held a more noble place in American history—and might even have been elected to another term—had it not been for the war in Vietnam. He approached the war with the same egotism, arrogance, and vindictiveness with which he dealt with domestic issues. One night at Camp David, the two of us leaning against its beautiful stone fireplace, I said to him, "This damned Vietnam War. We can't win it. If somehow we did win it, we would not have won anything. And carrying it on is killing a lot of young Americans who deserve better. Why don't you end it?"

He replied, "I'm not going to be the first American president to lose a war."

It was not Johnson's war. Eisenhower had put us into it, and Kennedy had carried it on. Johnson stuck with the judgments military leaders had given him that the Vietnamese were poor, physically inferior, badly armed and trained, wore sandals cut from automobile tires, had no air force. A think tank in Britain reportedly simulated the war by entering every fact about America and Vietnam into its computer. The result was that the United States won the war in thirty-six hours. Of course, a computer, or politicians and generals, can't predict everything that will happen in a war, but Johnson always chose to believe the most encouraging reports. He also feared bitter right-wing vengeance if he abandoned the war, and he knew the trouble that lay in wait for any Democrat who allowed another country to fall to Communism. He remembered too well what had happened to Truman on China and Korea.

But the same stubbornness that had worked so well for him in other times kept us in the war, and it almost surely cost him another term as president. One reason the public turned against the war was that it was the first war ever seen on television.

They heard an American captain who had just overseen the destruction of a village say that "We had to destroy it to save it."

They also saw and heard a handsome black soldier with a wounded leg being carried out on a stretcher screaming in agony, "Don't bend it!"

Many of the North Vietnamese did wear rubber-tire sandals, but we were fighting in their territory, not ours. It was in a jungle where they could easily hide. We couldn't get at them, couldn't see them. And when we found them, we didn't know whether they were North Vietnamese or South Vietnamese, Communists or anti-Communists, because they all looked and dressed more or less alike. One officer told me, "When we'd capture prisoners, we never knew what we had captured." But Johnson kept sending more troops. And the military began using all kinds of heavy-duty weapons, which were largely useless in a jungle with the enemy scattered all over. We were using $25,000 bombs to blow up $50 oxcarts.

World War II had a purpose. You could argue that the Korean War and the Gulf War and the Kosovo War and the post–September 2001 war on terrorism each had at least some kind of legitimate rationale. But I came to believe that the only purpose the Vietnam War had was for Johnson to be able to say that he did not lose a war so that he could win a second term. In 1966, when most of the American public was still supporting the war, I gave a speech at Ohio State University in which I said that what we were doing in Vietnam was "an endless, pointless, futureless exercise. We are not going to achieve anything substantial. We should try to wind up the war and get out of the tragic and costly burden." I took some criticism for that, but I also received several letters from people thanking me for taking a stand against the war when many members of the media were reluctant to voice their own opposition. On *The Huntley-Brinkley Report,* I started to express doubts about the war, and I insisted that we show it for what it was. We always reported skeptically the Pentagon's "body counts," which have since been shown to have been highly exaggerated.

When I began to oppose the war, Johnson turned against me personally. At first he just stopped having anything to do with me—no more invitations to Camp David for the weekend or to the White House for drinks. He was probably afraid to attack me publicly, because he knew that it would sound petty and vindictive and make him even less popular than he was. So he attacked me covertly, by telling people in private that by opposing the president and the armed forces I was hurting the country. And then I found out from someone in the White House that he had tapped my phones. I was furious. My first thought was to go on the air and say that my phone was tapped and "if you want to get a message to President Johnson, just call this number and he will hear it." But NBC talked me out of it, so I never did anything. Russell Baker, who was then at the *New York Times,* told me that when my phone rang I should pick it up and say, "Lyndon Johnson is the greatest president we have ever had in this country."

With Johnson's exit in disgrace from the national scene and the growing strength of American conservatism that he did much to cause, another period of social advance began to fade away. And so our march toward utopia was delayed again. But even those of us who believe in ensuring equality of opportunity and who feel it is the government's duty to give us service and protection—but not necessarily happiness—found no reason to be sorry. A great many valuable, important reforms were enacted during Johnson's presidency: Medicare, Medicaid, more funding for education, public housing, and transportation, civil rights and voting rights laws that helped create equality of opportunity. But by the end of his term in office it seemed to many that reasonable, non-utopian measures like these were the extent of what government should do. And it also appeared to most Americans that the war in Vietnam was a terrible waste of men and money. Johnson's failure to end it was what destroyed his presidency.

There is today on the Mall in Washington a monument listing the names of all those killed in Vietnam. Of all the marble and granite statuary lying between the Lincoln Memorial and the Washington Monument, it is the most moving and affecting. Many people who stop to examine it burst into tears. I wonder how many of them think of Lyndon Johnson when they do.

Bobby Kennedy

I never shared in the love affair that so many Americans—and so many members of my own generation in particular—had with John F. Kennedy. I liked Kennedy pretty well, and I liked most of what he tried to do in his short presidency. But there were a lot of things about him that I found unappealing—his father, Joe, for one, who was a character out of Dickens, a ruthless schemer who would do anything, moral or immoral, legal or illegal, to advance the fortunes of his family. Jack Kennedy could never have reached the presidency without him, and I didn't much care for the idea of a national leader being created, in effect, by his family's money and influence. I didn't approve of his friendship with Joe McCarthy, which he never really repudiated even during the worst of McCarthy's rampages. McCarthy was a friend of Joe Kennedy, and Jack

Kennedy was never one to turn against his father's friends. I didn't appreciate the self-celebratory tribal quality of the Kennedy family, their expectation that everyone they befriended would somehow serve their interests. And I didn't like what I saw (which at the time was not very much compared to what we now know) of Jack Kennedy's seamy personal life.

But Kennedy was smart and usually interesting and genuinely charming, not in the glad-handing way that Clinton was, but in a slightly reserved and even ironic way that I found appealing. He was a good speaker and in the short time he was in office a pretty good president. Like everyone else, I was shocked and saddened by his death, both because it was such a blow to our national self-image and because I liked him. But, to me, he was never the shining symbol of idealism and hope that he was to so many others.

The Kennedy brother I was closest to was Bobby. He was very different from his brother, and on the surface much less likable. Many people who were enamored with John Kennedy hated Bobby, most famously Lyndon Johnson. Bobby was younger and smaller, and within the family the boy from whom perhaps the least was expected. (In Joe Kennedy's family, nothing at all was expected of the girls, except that they behave themselves and marry; and the boys received attention to a large degree in proportion to Joe's expectations of their futures.) Jack Kennedy had a smooth, even serene public image—witty, ironic, self-confident, slightly aloof. Bobby was more rough-edged, hyper and intense. He didn't have his brother's relaxed public posture and easy wit, or his ability to charm everyone he met. Beneath the surface, Jack Kennedy may have been as intensely ambitious as anyone in his family, but Bobby was the one who showed it. He was ambitious for his brother more than himself, at least at first, and he was the bad cop in Jack Kennedy's presidential campaign. That was one reason why he had a reputation for being ruthless. He did the dirty work that Jack didn't want to do, and maybe didn't even want to know about. But he could be ruthless in other ways, too—as in his pursuit of Jimmy Hoffa, which (however much it might have been justified by Hoffa's underworld style of unionism) always seemed to me uncomfortably like a personal vendetta.

But Bobby was also different from Jack in other ways. President Kennedy enjoyed a reputation as something of an intellectual. He enjoyed smart people around him, and he cultivated writers and artists. When he gave speeches, he wanted to throw in quotations from great thinkers. Bobby was not entirely comfortable in the glittering world of artists and intellectuals. That was ironic, in a way. Jack Kennedy was not actually very much interested in the world of ideas and high culture, although he could pretend to be pretty effectively. But Bobby *was* genuinely interested. He never pretended to be an intellectual himself, but he loved listening to smart people and reading what they wrote. He organized seminars at Hickory Hill, his home in McLean, Virginia, and invited scholars and experts to come educate him and his guests on topics he thought were important. I went to a few of them, and I always learned something useful.

My first wife and I became quite friendly with Bobby and Ethel in the early 1960s and socialized with them and their very large circle a fair amount. There was a naively carefree quality about those years, despite the great world crises around us, and it showed in the gatherings and parties that the Kennedys gave or inspired—some of them in our house in Chevy Chase. Bobby in private was not the ruthless enforcer that he so often seemed to be in his public role. Like the rest of his family, he liked informality. Parties at Hickory Hill were usually large and noisy and filled with kids, with meals served somewhat haphazardly. Bobby worked in his office (first in the Justice Department, later in the Senate) in shirtsleeves, often accompanied by a big shaggy dog he'd brought from home. He was soft-spoken, a little shy, his hair always out of place, his clothes a bit disheveled. There was always a feeling of intensity just below the surface. He could joke and flirt and engage in small talk, but he usually moved on to something serious pretty quickly and bored in on you for answers to questions he thought you might understand.

I don't think Bobby was much interested in the normal responsibilities of the attorney general. It seemed to me that the Justice Department was run mostly by his deputies, except in those few areas in which Bobby took a particular interest, such as racketeering and Hoffa. Partly this was because he was so often at the White House and so engaged with all aspects of his brother's presidency. John Kennedy was one of the last presidents not to have a chief of staff, but in some ways Bobby played that role. He was the last line of defense between the president and the rest of the government. During the Cuban Missile Crisis, he was the man whom the president listened to most, the one who challenged the CIA and the Pentagon most often.

Bobby was devastated by his brother's death, in ways that went beyond normal grief. His life, as he understood it, had been built for so long around advancing John Kennedy's career that it took him a long time to begin to think he could have a career of his own. I believe it was also hard for him, having been so close to the center of power, to think of working his way up from the outside. Maybe that was why he hoped so desperately, and un-realistically, to be Lyndon Johnson's vice president (and thus his presumed successor) in 1964, even though he disliked Johnson and Johnson disliked him. Maybe that was also why, when he finally, and somewhat hesitantly, agreed to run for the Senate in New York, he never appeared to develop much interest in New York politics or in the ordinary work of the Senate. He was, after the president, the most famous politician in America, and even if he'd wanted to, he could not really have become a member of the Senate club in the way his brother Ted did.

The strangest and most interesting part of Bobby's life may have been the last two years or so before his death. In the 1950s and early '60s, he had been the ultimate Cold Warrior. Even more than Jack, he had been close to Joe McCarthy and had worked on the staff of his investigating committee during the height of the Red Scare. (In the end, he turned on the senator and used his inside knowledge of his tactics to help bring McCarthy down—an act for which my sister, who had been McCarthy's personal secretary, never forgave him.) When his brother was in the White House, it was Bobby who tried to fight off the civil rights movement and all other political and popular demands that might embarrass the president and distract attention from the foreign policy initiatives that Jack Kennedy was mostly interested in. He was furious with the Freedom Riders in 1961, and was only a little more sympathetic to the civil rights movement when he ordered federal marshals into Alabama in 1963 to force George Wallace to integrate the University of Alabama. When Johnson became president, Bobby wasn't much interested for a while in the domestic policies of the new administration, but complained constantly about how he thought Johnson was undermining his brother's foreign policies.

A few months after the president's assassination, we had a group of people from the Kennedy circle over to our house, including a lot of family members. Jacqueline was there, still in mourning, but dressed in white, subdued but clearly glad to be out in the world. Teddy and Joan were there, the most openly sociable of the bunch. Bobby and Ethel came too. Ethel by then had gotten used to being the outgoing half of the family, covering up for Bobby's depression, and she circulated through the house talking to everyone. Bobby secluded himself in our library and spoke with a few people, including me. He was then on the verge of resigning from the Justice Department to run for the Senate, and he was worried about how he would have a voice in foreign policy once he was out of the administration. By then Johnson was pushing through John Kennedy's civil rights bill and starting his own War on Poverty, but Bobby didn't yet seem to have very much interest in those issues.

Bobby did not have an entirely easy time getting elected to the Senate from New York. A lot of people there resented his entering the race after having had no previous interest in New York politics. (He had lived there awhile as a child, but not for many years after that.) The incumbent senator, Kenneth Keating, was a respected moderate Republican who probably would have been easily re-elected against any other opponent. He attacked Kennedy as a carpetbagger, with considerable effect. What probably turned the campaign decisively in Kennedy's favor was Lyndon Johnson's energetic campaigning with him in New York in the last weeks. But that did not do anything to dampen the personal dislike the two men had for each other. On election night in Austin, Texas, Johnson spent the evening watching himself being elected by one of the greatest landslides in history, but what most affected him, according to some around him, was watching Bobby Kennedy acknowledge his victory in New York without thanking the president for his support or congratulating him on his victory.

Over the next few years, Bobby seemed to transform himself. He threw himself into the roiling social movements of the sixties and began to criticize the Johnson administration for the same kind of caution and restraint that he and Jack had usually shown when his brother was in office. It was people on Bobby's staff who pushed through the idea of "community action" as a centerpiece of Johnson's War on Poverty—the basis of the program that gave people in the community control over programs set up to help them and that produced all sorts of controversy and scandal. Bobby even raised money for a war on poverty of his own in the Bedford-Stuyvesant section of New York. He became a friend and ally of Cesar Chavez, the head of the migrant farmworkers' union in California. That made Bobby the first major national politician to identify himself clearly with Hispanics. He was a passionate promoter of civil rights and racial progress, advocating programs far more radical than any his brother had ever considered. And he developed a large following among African Americans and other minorities.

I always wondered what drove him in that direction, which seemed to me such a change from his earlier politics. Part of it was undoubtedly ambition. He wanted to set himself up as the alternative to Johnson in the Democratic Party, and to do so in those years he had no choice but to move to Johnson's left. But I never believed that it was just ambition. Bobby was too passionate about what he did to do it purely through calculation. He had to make himself believe in the policies he was promoting, and he did. He could see how fast the world around him was changing, and given his own temperament, he could see that he had a choice—that he had to jump one way or the other. He could appeal to the fears and resentments of those who thought the changes were coming too fast and too recklessly, as Nixon and Wallace and others did. Or he could identify himself with the changes and try to lead them, and that's what he decided to do. Straddling the fence was not in his nature.

But in many ways the most startling change was his position on the war in Vietnam. Jack Kennedy had consistently increased American involvement in Vietnam; had helped orchestrate a coup in Saigon that killed President Diem and his brother; had sent tens of thousands of military "advisors" into the country; and had surrounded himself with advisors who kept pushing him to do more. Bobby never showed any discomfort with these policies while his brother was president, and the men who advised Johnson to escalate further were the same men Jack had appointed. A lot of John Kennedy admirers now argue that he would have withdrawn from the war after the 1964 election if he had lived. I've never seen much evidence to support that. Chet Huntley and I did an interview with President Kennedy in the White House not long before he died, and when we asked him about Vietnam, he was firmly committed to defending the South Vietnamese government. Bobby said very little about the war as the escalation continued in 1964 and early 1965.

But by the end of 1965, he was turning against the war, and by 1966 he was the most prominent critic of Johnson's policies in the country. He did not advocate unilateral withdrawal from Vietnam. Almost none of the mainstream critics of the war—including Eugene McCarthy—proposed that, even in 1968. (One exception was Senator George Aiken, whose solution to the war I always liked. He said we should simply declare victory and come home.) Kennedy advocated a bombing halt and negotiations, but the important thing about his stance (and that of McCarthy and others) was his clear belief that the war was a mistake and that we should be trying to end it as quickly as possible, not expand it.

Bobby was still reluctant to challenge Johnson directly. He was afraid he would be accused of ruthless ambition, of acting out of a personal grudge. And he was probably a little afraid of Johnson, too; Johnson could be very vindictive. So he refused to run against Johnson in the 1968 primaries, which is why antiwar leaders like Allard Lowenstein went looking for

another candidate and found Gene Mc-
Carthy. But it couldn't have been easy for
Bobby to stay on the sidelines, watching
the campaign develop and the antiwar
movement grow. As soon as McCarthy
showed how vulnerable Johnson was, almost defeating him in the New Hampshire
primary, Kennedy jumped into the race. I
saw him not long after he announced (one
of the last times I saw him, since he was
rarely in Washington after that), and he
told me he thought he couldn't stay out
and be true to his beliefs, even though he
knew that challenging McCarthy's claim to
leadership of the antiwar forces would
open him up to a lot of abuse—and it did.

Kennedy's campaign that spring was an
amazing thing to watch—especially the
passions it produced. The crowds swarmed
around this slight, shy, slightly boyish-
looking man, struggling to touch him,
grabbing his cufflinks and even his buttons
as souvenirs. He was never a particularly
good speaker—much less eloquent than
Jack, not even as good as Ted at his best—
but his audiences responded to him as if he
were a great orator. On the terrible day in
April when Martin Luther King Jr. died,
his short, moving speech in downtown In-
dianapolis, in which he quoted Aeschylus
to his poor, mostly black audience, was the

best and most powerful reaction I heard from anyone that day.

It was ironic that in this campaign Kennedy, who had grown up wealthy and privileged, the son of one of the richest and most powerful men in America, who had served as attorney general and a United States senator, saw himself as the anti-establishment candidate. But in many ways he was. Lyndon Johnson, having pulled out of the race himself, was doing everything he could to make sure Bobby was not the nominee and was lining up the party bosses behind Hubert Humphrey (whom Johnson didn't much like either, but greatly preferred to Kennedy). "I've got every establishment in America against me," Bobby said at one point. "I want to work for all those who are not represented. I want to be their president." Nice rhetoric, but I also think he had come to believe it. And that's one of the things that made him such a magnetic (and controversial) candidate.

Much of the political establishment did turn against him, lining up so many delegates for Humphrey that even though Kennedy won every primary he entered but one, it appeared that Humphrey—who ran in no primaries—would still have enough delegates to get the nomination.

That could not happen today, of course, when almost every state has a primary. But in 1968, most of the convention delegates were still chosen by the state political leaders. Kennedy thought that if he kept winning big primaries—California, New York, and so on—he could persuade the bosses to change their minds, convince them that no one but he would have a chance to win. But he didn't have time to find out if the strategy would work.

On June 4, I was in New York to broadcast the nightly news with Huntley and then to do a special report on the California and South Dakota primaries that were being held that day. Only a week before, Kennedy had lost the Oregon primary to McCarthy—the first time any Kennedy had lost any election. So it was vital to him to come back and win California. For a while it seemed as though McCarthy would have enough momentum to overtake him there, too, but Kennedy ran a good campaign and, in their one debate, clearly beat McCarthy, who was at his sarcastic and self-righteous worst. On election night, Kennedy won decisively (although not as overwhelmingly as he wanted)—46 percent of the vote, five points ahead of McCarthy, with the state attorney general, who was pledged to

Humphrey, getting the rest. (He also took South Dakota.) He gave a good speech that night in the ballroom of the Ambassador Hotel, clearly trying to reach out to McCarthy supporters and make himself the only real alternative to Humphrey—"not for myself, but for the cause and the ideas which moved you to begin this great popular movement." A few minutes later, as he was walking through the hotel kitchen, he was shot.

It was the middle of the night in New York, and I was already off the air. We went back on as soon as we heard the news and stayed on until the next morning, when we heard that Kennedy had died. I stayed in New York to cover the story, but I also spent some time with the Kennedy family when they arrived from California with Bobby's coffin. It was sometimes hard, once I found myself in the middle of that big, talkative, driven family, surrounded by what seemed like dozens of kids, to remember that everyone was there because of a great personal and national tragedy. They kept up a good front, maybe just out of habit, because there seemed no way to express what they really felt. I stood for a while as one of the honorary pallbearers watching over the coffin in

St. Patrick's Cathedral, and I can't even remember now how I felt that day.

On the day of the funeral, I returned to Washington. The ceremony was in New York at St. Patrick's, but the funeral party boarded a train to bring the body back to Washington for burial next to President Kennedy in Arlington Cemetery. It was like a scene out of the nineteenth century: people lining the tracks all the way from New York to Washington just to see the train go by, perhaps getting a glimpse of the flag over the coffin as the last car went by. The crowds were so large that the train had to move at a snail's pace, so that it was already getting dark by the time it got to Washington. Hundreds of people walked behind the coffin across Memorial Bridge and up into Arlington Cemetery, carrying candles. The pallbearers, two of whom were Bobby's sons, stumbled a little in the dark trying to find their way to the grave site. It was all I could do, seeing those kids carrying their father's coffin, to keep my composure on the air.

In a way, Bobby Kennedy's death—because it came after Jack's and after Martin Luther King's—was not as great a shock to many people as the earlier assassinations. A lot of younger Americans, in particular, had already decided that America was sick and violent and assumed that things like this were now the norm. But to me, Bobby's death was the hardest of all to take, partly because he was my friend, but also because I had never previously believed that the country was really in serious trouble. I had always thought that there were enough smart people with enough goodwill to pull us out of the mess we were in. And the shooting of Bobby Kennedy caused me for the first time to wonder if that was true. Sometimes I still do.

Ronald Reagan

I covered eleven presidents during my years in Washington, and knew all of them to some degree. But none of them remained as mysterious to me as Ronald Reagan. He was one of the great figures of his time, a president so well suited to the television age, so self-assured and friendly and attractive, that even his political enemies expressed at least grudging admiration for him. Speaker Tip O'Neill, who battled with him all the time, once said that Reagan "wouldn't have been much as a prime minister, but he would've made a hell of a king."

Few presidents have been as well served by the people surrounding them as Reagan was. He had talented people who worked hard to create an image of him as a leader who knew exactly what he was doing. James Baker, who was his chief of staff in his first term, was a great spokesman for

Reagan, always putting the president's actions in their most favorable light. His tax cut, Baker once said, was a "riverboat gamble that worked." Reagan, he said, "focuses on the big picture. He doesn't lose the forest for the trees." Budget director David Stockman, after giving an interview in *The Atlantic* in which he said the administration never was serious about closing the deficit, that the tax cut was a "Trojan horse," came out of a meeting with his famously amiable boss and said, clearly coached by someone, that it had been "like a visit to the woodshed." Reagan's White House advisor Pat Buchanan, not yet the maverick of the right he later became, could always be counted on to talk about Reagan's place in history. "All over the world," he liked to say, "they're cutting taxes. All over the world, they're talking about the private sector. All over the world they're cutting the size and growth of government. This is a direct consequence of Ronald Reagan the revolutionary."

Like most presidents, Reagan did less well in his second term as his more talented advisors left. His new chief of staff, Donald Regan, was remarkably clumsy in explaining what the president was doing—and then, after Reagan fired him, wrote a bitter memoir attacking the First Lady. During the Iran-Contra scandal, Regan said something that he may actually have believed would help the president, although no one else did: "Does a bank president know whether a teller in the bank is fiddling with the till? No!" Those years—after the president's dramatic landslide re-election in 1984—were the years of his infamous visit to Bitburg (where he was snookered by Chancellor Kohl into laying a wreath in a cemetery containing the graves of SS members); of the arms-for-hostages scandal, which Reagan always claimed to know nothing about; and of his own slowly dimming capacities, which produced more and more public statements that no one took entirely seriously because they figured Reagan didn't really know what he was saying. "Most of the homeless are homeless by choice," he liked to say. The unemployed simply chose not to work, he claimed, because he himself could see in the want ads of the *Washington Post* that there were plenty of jobs waiting out there for someone to take.

A few months before he left office, I sat with him in the Oval Office for about an hour and asked him about his presidency and his views on all sorts of things. One of the things I asked him was what it had meant to be the first former actor to serve as president. He told me, "There have been times in this office when I wondered how you could do the job if you hadn't been an actor."

I had a lot of sympathy a few years later when Edmund Morris published his book on Reagan, *Dutch,* and explained that even after years of research and hundreds of hours in Reagan's presence, he was so baffled by the man—as far from understanding him at the end of the process as he had been at the beginning—that the only way he could make the book work was to create a fictional character (named Edmund Morris) to narrate Reagan's life for him. Not many people liked the book much, but Morris was certainly not alone in finding Reagan impenetrable. Reagan always seemed to me to be a man who filtered reality through a set of assumptions and preconceptions that he refused to question, someone who made the world explainable to himself by looking at it as though he were looking through the lens of a camera, focusing only on the things that confirmed what he thought. And maybe that was part of his greatness: his ability to convey a kind of certainty and consistency that the state of the world in his time didn't do much to support, but that people loved to hear anyway.

I didn't think much of some of the things Reagan did or proposed—"Star Wars" (the missile defense plan), aid to the Contras, ratcheting up the arms race to force the "Evil Empire" to do the same. But I never thought he did these things cynically. I think he really believed in them, really felt they would work, and thus stuck with them much longer than many other politicians would have done, even though many people had turned against them.

What was most important about Reagan, though, had very little to do with his personality, except to the considerable degree that his personality helped advance it. Reagan's presidency created a rare thing in Washington, a new political culture. Up until 1980, Washington was still running on the increasingly rusty engine that the New Deal had built in the 1930s and that Lyndon Johnson had tried to refurbish and refit in the 1960s. Few people in government dared to question the New Deal orthodoxies that regulation of capitalism, strong unions, welfare payments to the poor, and steep progressive taxation of the rich were the cornerstones of a good society. But Reagan and his people did question those things—all of them—and to some degree overturned them. The Reagan years were years of deregulation (a process that had begun in the 1970s but that accelerated in the 1980s). All sorts of previously regulated industries—airlines, utilities, oil companies, and others—were cut loose and sent out on their own. It was a time when unions were forced into retreat, beginning with Reagan's gutsy decision to fire striking air traffic controllers when their stupidly arrogant union leader called them out on an illegal strike. The Reagan years were years in which the welfare state—although not dismantled, certainly—lost whatever legitimacy it had in the eyes of most Americans and began its long march toward the 1996 reforms that put work at the center of public assistance. And in the Reagan years low taxes became an orthodoxy that eventually even most Democrats accepted, in which wealthy people began to be treated as important contributors to economic growth instead of bloated plutocrats. The same thing was happening in Britain and in other industrial societies in those years, but the United States—the biggest, richest, and most important capitalist nation in the world—was the leader of this important revolution, the "market revolution," as many people called it at the time.

Tip O'Neill once said that there was in the 1980s "a degree of selfishness in

America that I hold President Reagan responsible for." And there was a lot of greed then, and beyond—although perhaps not much more than there always is in America. But Reagan didn't see it that way. He and those around him believed that they had unleashed a new age of capitalist expansion by cutting the strings that were holding the economy down. And while many problems have not been solved by these changes, and many new problems have emerged as a result of them, I'm not sure the country isn't better off as a result.

Bill Clinton

Although I had heard a lot about Bill Clinton during the years he was governor of Arkansas, I got my first real look at him while I was anchoring the 1988 Democratic National Convention. Clinton gave the nominating speech for Michael Dukakis, and he spoke tediously and too long. By the end, no one (including me) was paying much attention, and many people (including me) concluded that Clinton—who had a reputation as an up-and-coming young governor—had no future in national politics. Not for the last time, we underestimated him.

In 1992, after he struggled through his scandal-plagued campaign and decisively defeated a president who only a year earlier had won a war and earned a 90 percent approval rating, I began to think that he had the capacity to be a great president. He was smart, with a serious interest in policy.

But he was also one of the best natural politicians I'd ever seen. No one in recent history, I thought, had come to the presidency with such an exceptional collection of talents, and I thought he might be a great success. I think now I may have overestimated him too.

Clinton was a guest on my Sunday morning show a few times during the campaign, but the first time I met him outside the studio was at a dinner a few weeks before his first inauguration at the Georgetown home of Kay Graham, longtime publisher of the *Washington Post*. This was a gathering of Washington insiders—journalists, power brokers, Democratic Party grandees, and others—a world Clinton had never been much a part of, but one he did not view with the same disdain and insecurity that Jimmy Carter (another outsider from the South) had shown. He charmed everyone. He talked about the image that so many Americans had of Washington as a nest of vipers, and he said he wanted to open up the city to the American people, but that he also wanted to make Americans more open to, and tolerant of, Washington. His tone was perfect.

A few weeks later, I was spending New Year's at an apartment we owned in South Florida, in a building where Senate minority leader Bob Dole also spent the holidays. We were friendly, and I tried to get a sense from him of what he expected from Clinton and how he would deal with him. Dole didn't say much, but I got the distinct impression that he both disliked Clinton and feared him. I didn't know then whether Dole was planning to run for president himself four years later, but I suspected he was. I could tell that he considered Clinton a dangerous opponent, and I sensed that he would try to ensure that Clinton was not too successful. I hadn't yet caught on to the ferocity of the Republican Party's (and the Republican right's) dislike of Clinton, or to how terrified they were that he might actually succeed. I assumed that Clinton would face a normal level of partisan rancor. But both houses of Congress were in Democratic hands, and it seemed likely that he would be able to get a lot done.

Looking back now over the eight years of his presidency, I find it hard not to be disappointed by how far Clinton's actual achievements fell below the initial expectations. This was partly his own fault. For all his brilliance, he was an undisciplined man—most notoriously in his personal behavior, but probably more importantly in his political commitments. He trimmed and adjusted and "triangulated" so much that after a while no one had much faith in anything he said. Unlike formidable Republicans like Nixon, Reagan, and (it seems) the second Bush, none of whom was elected by a landslide at first but all of whom acted as if they had been, Clinton (who was decisively elected, despite the 43 percent of the vote he received, with his party in control of Congress) acted like a minority president from the start. He tried to placate almost everyone. He backed away from friends and allies when they came under attack, failed to support people he appointed to office, and seemed more concerned about what his adversaries thought than with what his supporters did.

His first weeks in office gave signs of some of the problems that would plague his presidency. And like most of his problems, they were not all of his own doing. Gays in the military—the issue that dominated the beginning of his administration—emerged because he had promised during the campaign to end the ban and was asked about it in a press conference shortly after he took office. Clinton had not wanted to bring this issue up so soon, but once asked he had no choice. And so, before he had had any chance to negotiate a route to this goal with the military or to build up public support for it in case the military balked, he got drawn into an incredibly rancorous debate. He didn't help himself much with the compromise— "Don't ask, don't tell"—that he cobbled together. And it now appears that he didn't help the gay men and lesbians in the military much either. I remember Harry Truman desegregating the armed forces in the 1940s and, in effect, telling the military that he was the commander in chief and that they would have to do this whether they liked it or not. Clinton might have been defeated anyway, but I can't help feeling he would have been better off if he'd taken a strong and principled stand on this issue instead of waffling.

He also got caught in a series of embarrassing miniscandals over some of his first appointments: the Nannygate controversies that sank Zoe Baird and Kimba Wood as possible attorneys general; the flap over some controversial essays by Lani Guinier, whom he nominated to head the civil rights division of the Justice Department. Again, Clinton had no way of knowing about most of these problems in advance, but he cut his people loose so quickly that he helped create the impression that he would not fight for them, or his issues.

His first two years, which for most important presidents have been their most productive, were amazingly frustrating, and frustrated. Clinton got Congress to approve an important tax bill, which helped eliminate the huge deficits that had been in place since the early Reagan years. And he got the Senate to approve the NAFTA treaty, which much of his own party—including the president of the AFL-CIO, led by my good friend Lane Kirkland—opposed. But he didn't get much else of significance through Congress, and he failed most spectacularly in the most ambitious project of his presidency: national health insurance, which the administration bungled in so many ways that it's hard to imagine how anyone thought it could ever be passed, although many people did think so for a while. In 1994, he suffered one of the biggest setbacks a sitting president has ever experienced: a Republican sweep that gave the GOP control of both houses of Congress for the first time in forty years. For a while, almost everyone wrote him off as certain to be a one-term president.

But as we now know, Clinton—whatever his other flaws—is supremely talented at surviving. He was lucky, of course, that the Republican right overinterpreted the results of the 1994 election as a mandate for some of its most radical goals. And when the GOP shut down the federal government rather than compromise with the accommodating Clinton, it all but ensured that it would lose in 1996. But Clinton was smart, too, in his characteristically unprincipled way. Rather than fight the conservative tide, he rode with it—far enough to co-opt the Republicans, but never quite far enough to alienate the Democrats. Given the depth of the right's hatred of Clinton, and the take-no-prisoners strategy of the Republican leadership, it's hard to blame him too much for defending himself tactically in this way. But to hear a Democratic president who had recently proposed the biggest expansion of government responsibility since the New Deal say before Congress in 1995 that "the era of big government is over" was pretty hard to swallow.

I saw Clinton quite a few times while he was president, usually on social occasions where we exchanged pleasantries and little more. But I suppose my most important encounter with him came on the air the night of the 1996 election. Clinton won easily, of course, but given the way he ran it's not surprising that he brought few Democrats into Congress with him. Late that evening, he finally appeared in Little Rock to give a victory speech. It would be hard to imagine a more woodenly scripted, bloviated set of remarks—an endless string of banalities that dampened the enthusiasm even of the loyalists in Little Rock who had been waiting for hours to hear him. I was tired after a long day, and I wasn't paying enough attention to the control room. Thinking I was off the air, I turned to Peter Jennings and a few other colleagues and started talking about what a bore Clinton was. In fact, we were still on a live broadcast, and the whole late-night television audience (and, of course, the media, which never sleeps) heard me. I doubt that many people at ABC really disagreed with what I said, but a lot of people were upset that I had spoken so bluntly about the president on the air, especially on election night, when traditionally the candidates are handled gently. The network was slightly mollified by the avalanche of letters and telegrams they received praising me for "telling the truth." "Finally someone had the courage to say it," one of them commented. But I was embarrassed by what I had said, and even by the enthusiastic response to it. Clinton's election night speech was indeed pretty awful, but no one could really argue that he is a bore.

ABC had scheduled an interview for me with Clinton a few days after the election, and the White House made it known that it would go ahead if I apologized to the president for what I'd said. There were some behind-the-scenes negotiations about what I would say and when I would say it, but I felt I owed the president an apology, and so I did not resist. On the day of the interview, I was seated in a White House meeting room surrounded by cameramen doing what most people who deal with Clinton do: waiting. But after not too long a while, the president walked in and greeted me warmly. I started the interview by saying I had been tired on election night and had spoken thoughtlessly, that my remarks had been inappropriate and unfair. Clinton was gracious, said a few nice words about my career, and the interview proceeded—but no real news came out of it that day. It was the last time I ever spoke with him.

I had retired from broadcasting by the time the Monica Lewinsky scandal broke, so I experienced it the way most Americans did—reading the papers and watching the news. It did not particularly surprise me that Clinton had behaved so recklessly and shamefully. We had all heard many stories about him over the years, and this one was all too believable, despite his emphatic, unconvincing, finger-shaking denial. But Clinton was far from the worst offender of public morality ever to occupy the White House. His pathetic, skulking relationship with Lewinsky would have seemed tame to any number of other presidents. Just to name the ones we know about, there were Warren G. Harding, Lyndon Johnson, and most of all John Kennedy, whose promiscuity is now legendary and whose reputation among Americans has hardly suffered at all. Clinton deserved to be embarrassed by the tawdry relationship he had with an intern, but this was hardly something that should have concerned the legal system or the public world. I wasn't much troubled by his petty dishonesty before the Paula Jones grand jury; the case was purely political from the start and the deposition was a fishing expedition by the right (which was funding and running the case) for anything they could use to discredit him. Kenneth Starr and the independent counsel's office, frustrated after nearly four years of investigating the Clintons' Whitewater land dealings without finding anything of consequence, seized on this trivial matter to justify themselves—and ended up disgracing themselves. The self-righteousness of the Republican impeachment managers in the House was truly extraordinary to watch. The whole affair made me sick— Clinton's shabby, furtive behavior; the press's sensationalistic coverage; the vindictiveness of the prosecutors and the congressional leaders. After a long life watching and covering Washington and American politics, I felt relieved that I was away from it all and not obliged to tramp through the muck of the Lewinsky case.

The one gratifying aspect of this sordid affair was watching the way the American people, as measured by opinion polls, seemed to sort out the rights and wrongs of the case much better than the people who were actually handling it. They thought less of Clinton as a person because of it, but it did not affect their view of him as the president. They opposed the investigations and the impeachment from beginning to end, even voted out a surprising number of Republicans in the 1998 elections—and that is probably what saved Clinton finally.

What was there about Bill Clinton that produced such intense and visceral hatred among his opponents? I'd seen nothing like it since watching the conservatives' loathing of Franklin Roosevelt in the 1930s and 1940s—a loathing so great that some of them openly celebrated his death. But the hatred of Clinton is harder to explain. Unlike Roosevelt, Clinton rarely threatened conservatives with policies that they truly feared. Except for the 1993 tax increase, he pretty much accommodated business and the wealthy. He accepted much of the drift to the right that had defined American politics since the 1970s, and on the whole did little more than moderate its hard edges. He was certainly a more conservative president (on domestic issues, at least) than Nixon. Some argued that he was to the right of Goldwater. But of course the whole character of American politics has changed in the last thirty years, and no president, Republican or Democrat, is likely to be as liberal as, say, Lyndon Johnson anytime soon.

One source of the hatred of Clinton, I think, was the sense among many Americans, even among many who liked him, that he was slippery, insincere, and opportunistic, without a set of core beliefs that could be counted on to guide him. That was true of him, I think, but it doesn't differentiate him very much from most other politicians. Part of it, undoubtedly, was his wife, Hillary, whom I always liked and thought highly of. But to many Americans, she seemed a cold, ambitious, ruthless woman, and the president didn't help her image much by putting her in charge of the ill-fated health care plan. Part of it was the right's resentment at how successfully he co-opted (and to some degree defanged) their issues. And part of it was his time. Clinton was president in one of the most successful periods in modern American history—prosperous, stable, seemingly unchallenged, and as a result frivolous, gossipy, scandal-obsessed, and highly, even viciously partisan. And Bill Clinton—handsome, charming, gifted, maybe the most dazzling political talent of my lifetime—was a magnet for all the partisan anxieties and resentments and jealousies of his era, a magnet all the more powerful because his personal behavior seemed to mirror the seamy aspects of that time.

Eventually, I suspect, Clinton will be viewed as a better president than most now consider him. He conducted a pretty responsible foreign policy on the whole, in a time that was, as we now understand, a lot more dangerous than most people thought. He balanced the budget for the first (and perhaps last) time in a generation. He helped keep the economy strong and stable for an extraordinarily long time. He made some real achievements in domestic policy, even if they were a lot smaller than he dreamed of. And he fended off some of the most reckless policies of the far right at a time when no one thought he had the strength to do it. Not so bad, I think, in the end. But it was sure a bumpy ride.

PLACES

Normandy, 1944 and 1994

In the NBC Washington news bureau where I worked in the mid-1940s, we were accustomed to a fairly leisurely work schedule—a little news that came in during the night, mostly from the war fronts; a little more at noon in what was called the "Esso Report," and our heavy-duty programs with more detail and more famous commentators in the late afternoons around six. In the meantime, we tuned in the other stations around town to see if they had anything we did not, including the station with reports by Gabriel Heatter, who combined news with his promotion of a laxative: "If you're over thirty-five, as I am, you need Serutan, which is natures spelled backward." Of Heatter's nightly performance I can remember only one interesting fact: that at the end of every broadcast he ran to the men's room to change his underwear. Why? Nobody knew.

The more serious and useful news came from Lowell Thomas and then H. V. Kaltenborn, a talking machine like none known before or since. My mother said of him, "He must have been vaccinated with a Victrola needle." He could go on and on sounding wise and knowledgeable even when he had no facts whatsoever. On the day of the attack on Pearl Harbor, he came on the air soon after and said that the country was now at war, but that the war would be short, a few days at most, only until the U.S. Navy could cross the Pacific Ocean and "devastate the islands of Japan." He then went on with several minutes of palaver about the history of Japan, the emperor as an object of worship, and Japan's inability to fight a real war—filling time until, he hoped, some more solid information came in over the news wires. He did not know that much of the U.S. Pacific Fleet had been sunk or damaged at Pearl Harbor and that it would be months, even years, before America would have a navy big enough to push the Japanese out of the Pacific.

Almost three years later, Thomas, Kaltenborn, Heatter, and the others had another big story: D-day, the Allied invasion of France. We had known it was coming, but we hadn't known when, and so it was big news when reports began to crackle out of radios all over town, and all over the world, that the invasion had begun. I was excited by the news, like everyone else, but I was also thinking of the men I had served with in the army, wondering where they were and how they were doing. It wasn't until fifty years later that I found out.

I grew up in Wilmington, North Carolina—a pleasant little port on the Cape Fear River, near the ocean, and especially busy during the war. It's a very old town, dating from the early eighteenth century, with some grand old houses from before the Civil War still standing. It also has some poor, junky areas, not only—as might be predicted for a small southern city in the 1940s—for black people, but also for whites. One of the worst white neighborhoods was Dry Pond, a rough, tumbledown, raunchy part of town. Many of the young men in the neighborhood worked unloading heavy crates from the ships that docked in Wilmington. The rest of the population consisted mostly of taxi drivers, drinkers, and gamblers. Despite their tough, marginal lives, there was a core of pride in the residents of Dry Pond. They were unknown members of the American working class, but they worked hard, played hard, and fought hard. I learned this firsthand.

About a year before Pearl Harbor, when the draft was just beginning, I volunteered for the U.S. Army. This was long enough before America entered the war that some of the old, antiquated army traditions still had not disappeared. One of them was creating companies out of people from the same town or community. I was assigned to Company I of the 120th Infantry, which I found was full of Dry Ponders. The first lieutenant was Mike Hall, Doc Hall's son, and most of the men were working-class guys from the neighborhood. I didn't know very many of them, and I didn't have very much in common with most of them. I was sent to the unit because they needed somebody who could use a typewriter. So at the age of twenty, I became supply sergeant for the 200 members of Company I, giving them uniforms, ammunition, guns. I manipulated the supply records to get the Dry Ponders off the hook for army stuff they had lost or stolen. The word went down our line of tents that the new supply sergeant was not a Dry Ponder, but he was okay.

The 120th Infantry was a famous old company of foot soldiers, rifle-carrying, mud-slogging, sleeping-on-the-ground foot soldiers, fed on creamed chipped beef on toast almost every day. It had a great history. It had been in continuous existence since the eighteenth century, when it fought the British in the American Revolution. During the Civil War, the regiment was part of the Confederate army, and on July 3, 1863, when General George Pickett's famous charge at Gettysburg was finally stopped, the Tar Heels who later became part of the 120th were led by Lewis Armistead and continued to push their way up Cemetery Ridge to what became known as "the high tide" of the Confederacy. During World War I, the regiment landed in France and waged a heroic assault on the famous Hindenburg Line, which turned out to be the decisive blow against the German defenses. After World War I, having fought in some of the bloodiest battles in American history, the 120th was famous for having never retreated.

But in the years of peace between the two world wars, the 120th, and my company—like the rest of the army—had fallen on hard times and was starved for money. We were given rifles designed in 1910, slow and cumbersome to fire, and we were housed in tents. Each tent had a funnel-shaped stove for winter heat, and when we tried to build a fire we found the stoves produced not much heat but were very, very efficient at setting the tent on fire. In the tent next to mine was a company of horse cavalry, with their horses nearby; at night we heard a chorus of their snorting and whinnying.

We were stationed at Fort Jackson, South Carolina, where the army was assembling all its southern units. At the time, before we had to face the reality of war, we knew a little about the history of the 120th, and we had developed a similarly romantic view of ourselves. We liked to think that we were rugged, rifle-toting foot soldiers always on the front lines and always the first to die. Since our bravery was untested, we had a lot of it.

After about a year with Company I, the army medics told me I had a kidney ailment and gave me an honorable discharge. I later discovered they had misdiagnosed me, but that mistake may have saved my life. I went to work for the United Press in various cities around the South, and later moved to Washington for NBC. I pretty much lost touch with the men I'd known in Company I.

In June 1994, I went to Normandy with television film crews from ABC News to report on the fiftieth anniversary of the great invasion that, after years of blood and death, had led to the end of the war in Europe. A few weeks before, I went back to Wilmington to find some of my old army friends from Company I. They were old men by then, but they remembered what happened in the war more vividly than they remembered almost anything else in their lives.

Ira Kelly was our top sergeant, who, because I could type, had thought I was his secretary. He was thirty-eight when he landed in Normandy. "I felt the sooner we got over there the sooner it would be over," he recalled. Lawrie Brown was eighteen in 1941. He had weighed 110 pounds, so skinny the army wouldn't have him. But he didn't take no for an answer. "I bet I ate ten pounds of bananas, went back and they let me in." Clarence Marshler had been one of the proudest of the Dry Ponders. "I thought we could do anything, what with the men we had," he told me. Charlie Porter had joined Company I when he was twenty-one, for the same reason many other young men were signing up: "It was a job that had to be done," he said. "If we didn't stop Hitler, he was going to take us." But except for war movies, the young men in the company had never spilled, or even seen, any blood, and they had no idea what lay ahead of them in France. Frank Sullivan, who was twenty-three at the time, remembered that once they landed in France, "it scared the living daylights out of me, and I was scared all the way through."

When the Allies decided to concentrate on an invasion of Europe, the 120th Infantry was chosen as one of the units to lead the charge. In February 1944 the Dry Ponders of Company I, along with the rest of the 120th, boarded ships on the coast of Massachusetts and set off across the Atlantic. Twelve days later they arrived in Scotland, where they were put on trains and moved to a town on the coast of the English Channel. It was decided that the unit would land on Omaha Beach immediately after the initial assault. A few days before the invasion, the regimental commander spoke to the men:

We are the outstanding, and most trusted, infantry regiment in this Divi-

sion . . . For the future, I ask God to
bless you . . . that you come through
the ordeal ahead, safe and sound, with
your head high in the pride of victory.
For myself, I don't ask God for any special favor to protect me from death or
wounds, for instance, . . . but I do ask
Him, with my whole heart and soul, to
give me the moral, physical and mental
courage and strength to do my duty to
the utmost.

While the first wave of Allied soldiers
were landing on the Normandy beaches
in the early morning of June 6, the Dry
Ponders of Company I and the rest of the
120th Infantry were already preparing to
join the fighting. They hit Omaha Beach
on day 3 of the invasion. By then, the Germans had been driven from the beach to a
position a few miles behind the bluffs. The
beach was secure, but the body parts and
bloody sand gave the men of the 120th an
idea of what lay ahead.

The 101st Airborne, which had para-
chuted behind German lines the night before the initial invasion, amid incredible
chaos, was holding the front line behind
Omaha and Utah Beaches. After the 101st
had spent several days keeping the German
army at bay, General Omar Bradley, com-

mander of the First Army, of which the 120th was a part, decided it needed to be relieved. He called on the 120th to take control of the line. On June 13, the regiment arrived at the front line between the towns of Isigny and Caretan. Two days later, on June 15, the 120th got its first real taste of combat when it launched an assault on the Germans. The fighting that day was slow-going and bloody. Men were dying in order to gain only a few yards at a time.

The 120th managed to push two and a half miles south to within a few hundred yards of the important Vire-et-Taute Canal. From there, the regiment continued to move through the French countryside, pushing the Germans farther into the interior. The Third Battalion, which included Company I, made it to the small village of La Compte in the late morning. German artillery started booming down on them; land mines were exploding under the tanks; and some of the men were coming close to panic. Many of them couldn't sleep that night.

Over the next few days, Company I fought for control of the canal, and finally pushed the Germans back, even though it took some ferocious fighting to do so. At one point the Dry Ponders were picking up German grenades and flinging them back across the canal before they exploded. But once the canal was taken, things slowed down. Then, in early July, they started advancing toward the town of Saint-Lô, fighting off German tanks and flamethrowers. They captured Saint-Lô on July 18, although there wasn't much left of it by then—mostly rubble. Company I and the 120th Infantry marched down the main street, the Rue St. George, while the French residents stood on the sidewalks and clapped and cheered at seeing them come.

After leaving the town, the Germans dug themselves in along a line just south of Saint-Lô, and for a time no one could get them out. For the Allied high command, this was their worst nightmare. The generals remembered the long, terrible stalemate during World War I when both sides had entrenched themselves across the French countryside. They were not going to return to the endless trench warfare of the last war. General Bradley came up with a plan, code-named Cobra, designed to break through the new German line. Cobra would begin with a massive aerial bombardment of the German front near Saint-Lô, followed by a big infantry attack.

It was a risky plan, because the space separating the American and the German front lines was very narrow. The bombers would have to be precise to avoid hitting their own forces.

A little beyond Saint-Lô, the 120th Infantry was lined up near the north side of what is now a pretty country road, the Saint-Lô–Périers highway. The Germans were lined up on the other side. There was only about a mile between them. Bradley wanted the bombers to concentrate on that road, and planes from the Eighth Air Force took off from England on July 24. The weather was heavily overcast, and the commanders in England ordered the planes back. But a lot of the pilots didn't receive the message, and they continued over Normandy and tried to aim through the clouds at the road. They dropped almost seven hundred tons of high explosives. Some of it hit the Germans, but one of the bomber formations missed badly and dropped its load directly on the men of the 120th Infantry.

The surviving members of Company I remembered it well.

"This was something like I'd never seen before in my life," said Frank Sullivan. "You'd look up there and it was like rain, big drops of rain at first but they got bigger and bigger, and there were so many of them and when they hit the ground it just vibrated." The official count was 25 American dead, 131 wounded. Everyone was angry. Some of the American infantrymen fired at their own planes. General Bradley was especially furious. He had been told that the planes would come in parallel to the American front line to ensure the bombs would miss the friendly troops. But without notifying the army, the air corps changed its plans and made a perpendicular approach to the target.

The next day the weather was clear, and Bradley ordered another bombing run. This time the attack was even larger. Over two thousand bombers flew over Saint-Lô. "It was an awe-inspiring sight to see the big bombers approaching in tight formation from the north, filling the sky like a cloud of huge locusts," a lieutenant in the regiment recalled. At first, the bombs hit only Germans, and some of the Americans cheered. But after about thirty minutes, the wind shifted and blew smoke over the American troops so that it was impossible to tell the difference between the two sides. And so again, for the second time in two days, the air corps bombed the 120th Infantry. The great war correspondent Ernie Pyle was there and wrote about it:

And then all of an instant, the universe became filled with a gigantic rattling, as if huge, ripe seeds in a mammoth dry gourd. I doubt that any of us had ever heard that sound before, but instinct told us what it was . . . There is no description of the sound and fury of those bombs except to say it was chaos and a waiting for darkness. For it's an unnerving thing to be bombed by your own planes.

This second bombardment killed 111 Americans, including Lieutenant General Leslie McNair, who was only the second American general to die in combat during World War II. An officer who was near McNair at the time recalled that "a bomb . . . threw his body sixty feet and mangled it beyond recognition, except for the three stars on his collar." Four hundred ninety American soldiers were wounded. The 119th and 120th Infantries accounted for the bulk of the casualties, with 64 killed, 374 wounded, 60 missing, and 164 cases of "combat fatigue" between them. Many of these men were in my old Company I.

Years later, I received a letter from one of the bomber pilots after he saw me talk about this on television. He said he was sorry.

. . .

Despite the chaos, the surviving members of the 120th Infantry got the order to attack. And finally, after a long siege, they pierced the German defenses and the American breakout began. By early October, they were about to cross into Germany.

At that point, just about everyone, from the foot soldiers of Company I to the Allied high command, had decided that the war in Europe was almost over. But Hitler ordered one last desperate attack that he thought might still win the war (and that his generals thought might make it possible to obtain a negotiated peace instead of the unconditional surrender Roosevelt and Churchill were demanding). This was the Battle of the Bulge, in December 1944, in which the Germans drove into a "bulge" in the Allied line with a huge, last-ditch counterattack in the dead of winter. The 120th Infantry was there.

The night before they joined the battle, a corporal in Company I, whose name I never knew, went to an officer who was going to remain behind and was thus unlikely to be killed by the Germans and handed him forty-five American dollars in cash, all he had. He said that if he died in battle he wanted the officer to use the money to send his wife one rose every Friday. Two days before Christmas, as the Dry Ponders were settling in to the town of Malmedy, which they had just captured, the U.S. Air Corps—mistakenly believing that the Germans had retaken the town— started three days of heavy bombing. The corporal, and many other members of Company I, died. The officer kept his promise and sent the roses.

Learning about the Dry Ponders of Company I, and about the battles they had fought, was a moving experience for me. I had known these men well for a little while, but I had lost track of them when they went overseas and had mostly forgotten about them after that. Finding them again—both the dead and the living—reminded me of what an extraordinary sacrifice the men of their generation had made.

During my visit to Normandy in 1994, I took a walk through the Allied cemetery near Omaha Beach, where 9,386 American servicemen who died in France are buried, including about a hundred members of Company I. I realized that I was walking through American history, among soldiers who did not live to see how good they were or how well they fought. Nor did they live to see the country, and the world, they saved. For those too young to remember all of this, it's an abstraction, an event you have heard about but did not see. But it is not abstract when you walk through that cemetery and find the name of a friend from army days, from the 120th Infantry or Company I or Dry Pond, his name engraved on a white marble cross.

Then it's real.

The Mediterranean

Being a news anchor, as I was for more than twenty years, involves a lot of sitting behind a desk. I loved the job, but at times I needed to get away from the office and the studio and see something of the world I was reporting on every night. And so beginning in the late 1950s, I made a series of documentaries for NBC about a number of interesting and sometimes exotic places. They were among the first major travel documentaries ever broadcast on television (although later, of course, there would be many), and so those of us who worked on them, having never done or even seen anything like these films before, felt in a way like we were making home movies— the world's most expensive home movies. They weren't really travelogues, but they certainly weren't conventional news either.

Over the years, I made a half dozen or so of these films, all of them with a title that began "Our Man in . . . ," after an old British newspaper term for foreign correspondents. The first one, broadcast in 1959, was "Our Man in the Mediterranean." Looking back on these films today, thirty to forty years after I made them, I realize that what we were doing—although we didn't know it at the time—was capturing some aspects of life in parts of the world that were in the midst of enormous change. Countries not yet fully a part of global culture and industrialization; not yet transformed by the enormous population explosions that were just starting; not yet overwhelmed by pollution or by democratic or antidemocratic revolutions or by religious fanaticism. But a decade or so after World War II, these countries were already beginning to experience at least some of these changes. So in making these films, we were trying to show something of the history of western civilization, but we were also capturing a moment in that history in which these societies were beginning to change forever.

My idea for a documentary on the Mediterranean would probably seem unfashionable today. It was to take a look at the countries from which what we now think of as western civilization emerged: Egypt, Israel, Greece, Italy, Spain. We took our camera crew and our credit cards to eight countries bordering the Mediterranean, where we tried to portray a sense of an area that was the middle of the ancient world and the birthplace of ours. I discovered that the places we visited were so full of the things that define our own civilization, that determine who and what we are, that I often felt like a grown man who had come back to walk around in the town he was born in. It was remote and strange, and yet somehow it seemed I had been there before.

We began in Egypt, where we went to the Sahara and shot footage of me, clad in a standard American business suit, riding a camel to lunch. We had hired a local man to pitch a tent and serve a more or less authentic Bedouin-style lunch out in the desert. There were faster and better-smelling ways to travel than on a camel gangling across the hot sands, but there was nothing much cheaper: a camel rented for two dollars and twenty cents a day. The caterer, if you can call him that, was a type easy to find in Egypt, in fact, a type hard to avoid—if he couldn't sell you one thing he would offer you another: a roll of film, postcards, a horse, a sightseeing trip, a belly dancer, a donkey, a goat, an Arab musical band, or a lunch in the desert. We hired the camels, the lunch, and the band. The food was all the ancient mystery of the Middle East, wrapped in grape leaves and very good, even after a little sand blew in it.

Near the Nile, we shot footage of an Egyptian water wheel in operation. Though the scene was from 1959 A.D, it could have been from 1959 B.C., because nothing had changed since then. Nothing. The wheel was hand-carved from palm and acacia wood and a blindfolded ox pushed it in circles, exactly as pictured on stone tablets from the age of the pharaohs. Its creaks and groans had echoed down the valley of the Nile for five thousand years.

In downtown Cairo we found a more complicated picture. At first glance the capital seemed shiny and modern, but it quickly became apparent that all the steel and concrete was just a new cover over an old and spoiled fish. When Gamal Abdel Nasser and his nationalist friends in 1952 drove out the greedy and obscene King Farouk, they exposed the enormity of Egypt's corruption, dirt, disease, and igno-rance. What had seemed to the world's ro-mantics to be the place to float exquisitely down the Nile on a barge and dally on the terrace at the Shepherd's Hotel was shown actually to be a place where a new baby's life expectancy was thirty-seven years, where eight out of ten could neither read nor write, 2 percent of the people got 50 percent of the income, blind beggars clogged the streets, the average income was less than two dollars a week, major and minor corruption was a way of life, and where, except in a few cities, living standards were the lowest on earth. After seven years of Nasser, there were more schools, some land reform, and some people were allowed to vote. But Nasser still appealed to the street mobs with the familiar tricks of the demagogue, hatred and abuse of foreigners, and the fiction that the ailments of seventy million Arabs were caused by two million Israelis. He also went after the flashy and external symbols of progress: new steel bridges for people to ride across on donkeys and to sail under in ancient and tattered feluccas, and a military force out of all proportion to Egypt's size and income.

Another showy, external symbol was a new Hilton Hotel recently built with Egyptian money in downtown Cairo. The architecture was Miami Beach revival. We were there on the day the Hilton was opened, along with Yugoslavia's Marshal Tito, who happened to be passing through on his way home from a youth rally. It was a sign of Egypt's eagerness to show off its frail connection to the "modern" world that Nasser himself came to the hotel opening. He and hotel man Conrad Hilton invited Tito to come on over to the new place and meet the folks from Broadway and Hollywood who had also been invited. We tagged along. The celebrities included Hugh O'Brian (television's Wyatt Earp), who was between cowboy pictures, the actor Van Johnson, some Broadway journalists, and assorted junketeers. Nasser said he liked the hotel fine, but he did think the bathrooms were a little snug for a man his size. Tito said something vague about maybe having a Hilton Hotel in Belgrade. There was a good deal of milling about, pouring of coffee, a lot of spilling and dropping of things, swapping of autographs. There was also a full program of organized entertainment: a fashion show featuring clothes of what was described as "pharaonic," or early Egyptian, styling.

Eventually the entire cast of hundreds was gathered into buses and cars and driven out to a nearby desert, for Arab foods and more entertainment in a tent. As they arrived at the base of the pyramids, the more experienced desert hands noted ominously that the wind was rising, but this did not faze their genial host, Conrad

Hilton. Leonard Lyons and other professional celebrities and celebrity watchers walked about beneath the Sphinx, which had seen many strange sights in its day. Hilton walked through wearing an Arab headpiece. As the wind and sand slowly rose, the cast gathered inside a rented tent. Sword dancers had a little trouble competing with the slapping and fluttering of the tent flaps and the flying sand, yet Hilton carried on, trying not to notice. Performer after performer appeared to entertain and beguile, one playing an Egyptian shell game with a baby chick, another a scantily clad but heavily bejeweled belly dancer. As the assembled crowd left the tent, one could see palm trees and movie stars bending before the wind, people with sand between their teeth, groping and leaning their way toward the buses, bringing to an end an episode in the Egyptian–American cultural exchange program.

From Egypt we headed north to Lebanon, at the extreme east end of the Mediterranean. When the Romans owned the Mediterranean they owned Lebanon too, only then it was known as Phoenicia. We visited Baalbek, a mountain town that still contains ruins of Roman temples. The Romans built the temples seventeen hundred years ago and what remains is more than just a sight. It's an experience no one who goes there can ever forget. "Ruins" is much too poor a word for this monument to man's energy and imagination, standing now in magnificence and utter silence. Nowhere on earth, not even in Rome itself, can the vitality and power of ancient Rome be seen so well. For westerners, whose heads are often full of withered schoolbook history, Baalbek makes the past seem alive. We have been taught that the Roman Empire declined and fell a dozen centuries ago, but we are so much products of that empire that standing in Baalbek is like standing in your own family churchyard.

Downtown Beirut, on the other hand, was as mid-twentieth-century as anything in the Middle East. That was in part because before the wars with Israel it had been a meeting place for the European and Arab worlds: American tourists in sensible shoes mingling with Arab oil billionaires with their coveys of Cadillacs and dancing girls. The ancient Phoenicians were the original traders. They took the ancient civilization of the Nile and the Levant and carried it west and made money out of it. Their descendants in Beirut did so as well, at least until the city became a bombed-out shell in the 1970s and 1980s. When we were there, Beirut was still the "Paris of the Middle East" and the commercial center of the region. In the city's bazaar you could buy anything, merchandise was constantly coming and going, east and west, by ship and by muscle, and dollars, pounds, francs, piasters, drachmas, dinars, lire, guilders, pesos, marks, and rubles were being bought and sold like cabbage.

The Egyptians are thought to have invented civilization, and the Lebanese, or more accurately, their Phoenician ancestors, to have carried it around the Mediterranean, but the Greeks created the idea of civilization as we have come to understand it. We discovered that this considerable achievement so overwhelmed them they have been talking about it ever since. The Romans in ancient times held a fixed opinion that the Greeks talked too much, that while they did a great deal they might have done more and survived longer if they had not at all times stood about in a dense, impenetrable fog of words. It is not historically accurate to relate a modern Greek too closely to a Greek of antiquity, because too many tribes and too many conquerors have been there since, but it was quite clear that the Greeks liked to talk then and they still liked to talk in 1959—

and they liked to talk most of all about their country's very distant past.

We took our camera to Constitution Square in Athens, the conversational capital of the country, maybe of the world. The Greeks have always preferred the streets to their homes, always preferred crowds to privacy, noise to silence, and conversation to quiet thought. In Constitution Square they had it all. The noise level was about like that in a small-mammal house on a hot afternoon. I noticed that the men sitting at café tables argued in a singular way. The purpose of having an argument was not to win; the purpose of an argument was to have an argument. They did not answer each other's points directly. Each made his own separate argument independent of the other. Each built his case in a straight vertical line, like two side by side Corinthian columns—the two of them going upward without ever meeting or touching. The idea was to build until your opponent could build no more. The winner, if there was a winner, was whoever built his column the higher and left his opponent below, not convinced and his mind not changed, but simply outbuilt. It might be illogical but it gave everybody a chance to talk, and that was the whole idea.

Greek Revival architecture in America is seen in government tax offices, big ugly boxes with a few Ionic or Corinthian columns across the front. Interestingly enough, we found the same kind of bad Greek Revival in Greece. The parliament building had the columns but it looked like a cold-storage plant, while the foreign office might have been a bank building in downtown Middle America. Thankfully, we also found the Greek heritage of taste surviving in wonderful ways. An American police traffic pedestal might have a sign starkly saying "Keep Right"; in Athens it was banded with a classic Greek key design. After touring the Acropolis, I was curious to see what the Greeks were building in the 1950s, so we went to look at a middle-income suburb, one that in the United States would be called Azalea Acres or Country Club Knolls. We discovered that stucco, tile, and grillwork doors had followed the sun and the thirty-year mortgage around the earth.

The Italians, on the other hand, have committed very few architectural outrages, and the monument, or eyesore, to King Victor Emmanuel II by the Forum in Rome only proves the point. One of our guidebooks described it as follows: "its gleaming white marble bristling with a spun-sugar icing of ornament, turret, and statuary looks for all the world like a spun-sugar confection." To me it looked less like a confection than a pile of used building materials. In front of this monstrosity is the Piazza Venezia, where Mussolini used to speak from his balcony and where we witnessed Rome's heaviest traffic. Buzzing scooters and roaring cars shot into the piazza from eight directions. The traffic was so thick, the Roman police put their best men here, specially trained for the job. The work was so taxing the officer had a half hour on, a half hour off. I was struck by the stylized movements of the traffic officers in the Piazza Venezia, which seemed so balletic that we accompanied the footage of them with a musical soundtrack.

In the darkling winter of 1820, the dying John Keats lived in Rome. There was really only one fitting and proper place in town for an English Romantic poet to perform his last act, a slow and tragic death in the days of his youth. Keats chose to die beside the Spanish Steps. There, he could see all of Rome in a little space. At the top of the steps is an ancient Catholic church, built when Columbus was sailing westward. Beside it, a relic from the Mediterranean's great days of international looting and robbery, an obelisk, covered with hieroglyphs, which the Romans stole and brought home from Cleopatra's Egypt. And Keats could see the steps, which are more than a way to go up and down: they are a quiet, stone cascade you can walk on. We found that the steps had also become a place where Romans and tourists came to admire it all and each other, to take snapshots, to sit and loaf, to sit and rest in the sun, and to look at the girls. In fact, it's very hard to walk up and down the Spanish Steps because they are so filled with people sitting on them. At the bottom of the steps we came across Babington's Tea Rooms. With Keats and others, this area became the English colony in Rome, so at Babington's you can get a suitable cup of tea and English digestive biscuits, suitably indigestible. Leading from the foot of the Spanish Steps is the most stylish and expensive shopping street in Rome, the Via Condotti. But for all the style and money one could see in Rome in 1959, there was still enough of the preindustrial past to make it clear that the city was still not fully in the twentieth century. When we visited, several local sculptors were raising their own chickens to feed themselves.

Also near the foot of the Spanish Steps is the smallest country in the world. It takes up just half an acre and is the only country located by street address, 68 Via Condotti. Tourists, particularly Americans, come to the steps without ever knowing there's another foreign country within a one-minute walk. It is the Sovereign Military Order of Malta, or SMOM, a Roman Catholic organization that runs hospitals around the world. We were so taken with it that we returned to SMOM a few years later and made it part of another documentary we did on the so-called "postage stamp" countries. Because of its location in a single building on an expensive shopping street in the high rent district of Rome, the country at the time of our visit was renting out its ground floor to a jeweler and a haberdasher. SMOM's almost total lack of geography is one reason it has been able to survive as long as it has, about nine hundred years. Whenever it has been threatened by a country of superior manpower—and there is no country that *doesn't* have superior manpower—it has just packed up and moved. It started in Jerusalem, then went to Malta, where it adopted the name and also the Maltese cross, and finally, in 1787, after eight moves, it settled down in Rome, where it has remained, protected by the Italian police and unmolested by the Italian tax collector. It issues its own passports, it has its own flag (red and white), it has its own automobile license plates, and at one time it had its own merchant marine—a small rented freighter—but it sank. As in every other country in the western world, it was a little hard around there to find a parking place, but that was the only problem they seemed to have. There was no farm crisis, no military budget, and no crime to speak of. The only full-time resident of the building was the concierge, who because he lived inside the confines of the country paid no taxes to anyone, which may have accounted for the wide smile he wore the entire time we were there. SMOM's foreign policy is to operate its hospitals around the world, to protect its faith, and generally to try to behave itself as a sovereign country. As standards of international conduct go, SMOM is a model citizen: quiet, well-behaved, and very neat.

Our next stop on the Mediterranean tour was Monaco, the most famous of the postage stamp countries. As far as I know, Monaco was then the only country in the world whose public information officer was also a Hollywood press agent, the same one Grace Kelly used when she was in the movies. When Kelly married Prince Rainier and moved into the palace, the agent kept the account. In Monaco we found a place where you could buy an apartment at Fifth Avenue prices, become a resident, and dodge taxes. You could rent a suite at the Hotel de Paris at an astronomical rate, or ride on a bus and buy a frozen custard for twenty cents. It was a place where you could rub elbows, if you wanted to, with maharajahs, croupiers, princes, postcard salesmen, archdukes, money changers, former Latin American dictators, rich ex–black marketers, Swiss and German businessmen, yachtsmen, and the cream of the world's jewel thieves.

We discovered slot machines scattered around the tiny principality, imported from the United States to skin low-income visitors. In the past, Monaco was unaware there were any low-income people. Mainly, the country was built with the gambling losses of Russian grand dukes who frequented the casino, which experienced its heyday before World War I. In those days there was genuine gold and glitter, because the wealth and titles and trappings were all present. By the time we paid a visit, you were more likely to see a player in Bermuda shorts at the roulette table betting a dollar. Gambling used to finance the country, but by 1959 it was bringing in only 4 percent of the budget. Still, we learned that the English church in Monaco never posted a hymn number lower than 36, because if it did, people would rush out of the church and go to the roulette wheel to play the number.

After an hour's drive down the Riviera we arrived in Cannes, where on the sand hauled in by the Carlton Hotel to smooth out the beach for its guests, we found people languidly pursuing the Riviera's foremost character-building exercise. In the days when peasants were tanned and the wealthy were pale, the Riviera was a winter resort, but somebody in the 1920s first combined the noun "sun" with the verb "bathe" and it became a summer resort. The really proper thing at Cannes was to take the sun in a private villa and to be tanned all over. The next best thing was to do it at the beach and be tanned nearly all over. The essence of the modern-day Riviera could be seen at the Cannes yacht basin, where the boats were intended for two kinds of people: those who wanted to sail around the Mediterranean and those who wouldn't dream of leaving the dock, because if the yacht was at sea, nobody would know they had it.

After lazing around Cannes, we crossed the Mediterranean and arrived in Algeria, on the northern coast of Africa, which was then undergoing a nationalist insurrection against French control that three years later, in 1962, led it to independence. The area was known as the Barbary Coast when the Arabs who occupied it went into the piracy trade. Hardly a ship could get by them. The English, in one three-year period, lost three hundred ships. That went on clear into the nineteenth century and nobody really tried to stop it until the brash new country to the west, America, became outraged and in 1815 sent Lieutenant Stephen Decatur here with a fleet to attack the pirates. He did, with some success, but the piracy wasn't really stopped until 1830, when the French came here to stay and the Barbary Coast became Algeria. There was nothing there then but the Casbah, an Arab city built on top of a Roman city. The city of Algiers grew up around it. I was eager to see the Casbah because so much had been written about it, mostly in romantic novels. Thus prepared, I was shocked to find it was a foul-smelling urban slum. On camera I said that if any young lady were invited by Charles Boyer or anyone else to come with him to the Casbah—don't go.

It was the 1938 movie *Algiers,* starring Boyer as a soft-eyed crook named Pepe Le Moko in love with Hedy Lamarr, that really gave the Casbah its reputation. The unromantic truth, regrettably, was that the Casbah was unspeakably filthy. In walking through it I felt a reluctance to touch anything and wondered if I really had had enough typhoid shots. When we visited, 85,000 people lived there in less than half a square mile, as many as a dozen to a room. Mostly the residents were unskilled laborers, dock workers, and street cleaners who worked outside the Casbah during the day, leaving the town to the women and great numbers of children. The French, with public health work, had lowered the infant mortality rate, but the birth rate had gone through the roof.

Until just before we arrived, the Casbah had been a center not only for dirt, but for banditry and assorted vices as well as nationalist rebels. But the French army went through every inch of it with flashlight, map, notebook, and tommy gun, until they knew who and where everybody was. The Casbah we saw had twenty-four-hour military guards and was totally under French control. The army's attitude there was curious. It was determined to subdue all of Algeria as it had subdued the Casbah, at gunpoint, but at the same time the people were often treated with care, even tenderness. They were shot full of penicillin, given chest X rays and schoolbooks. The

French were determined to control, and at the same time to uplift and improve, the population—colonialism in its waning, desperate-to-please days.

Outside the Casbah, Algiers was a thoroughly French city. Except for the large number of Arabs, the shape and flavor of things, the pace, the sounds, the food, the music, were all pure French. While the fight with the rebels went on in the deserts and hills outside, Algiers was reasonably quiet. However, there was an occasional shooting in the streets or an occasional rebel hand grenade that usually clattered around the cobblestones before exploding among women and children. The time of greatest danger was when the power failed and all the lights went out. Then the rebels poured into the streets with guns and bombs. But the French colonists were adamant. They would not give up, and they would not leave. They had lived there since 1830 and had built the city. Their lives and homes were there. They were there before the Americans crossed the Mississippi and opened the West. They had nowhere else to go. Three years later, when Algeria became independent, many of them did, in fact, leave—but not all.

In the center of Algiers we saw a tin-can city, a slum built of scrap wood and flattened tin cans, which was the first of a three-stage rehousing program on which the French were spending millions. It was in three stages, the French told us, because moving Arabs from slums directly to modern housing was impossible. The French claimed that the Arabs moved into the modern housing and didn't like it because it was too open and had too many windows. So the French moved them from the tin-can city to an intermediate housing project, substantially built, with a few small windows, which served as a sort of decompression chamber. The Arabs moved in there and stayed until they were used to it, and then into the new and modern housing developments.

The French were trying to subdue the rebels with gunfire where necessary and with peaceable means where possible, including building housing for the Arabs and letting them have it for six to eight dollars a month. In one housing development we visited, there were four thousand new apartments holding twenty thousand people, mostly children. The French officials told us they were trying to keep up but the Arab population was growing faster than they could put up the buildings. When I asked why they hadn't done all this long ago and maybe avoided some of their troubles now, they shrugged and said the important thing was that they were doing it now.

We left Algeria and moved west, because everything in the Mediterranean seems to have moved west, civilization and all the trade and money and ideas that go with it. The alphabet moved west, religions moved west. What we discovered was that the Mediterranean was a pond with everything on each of its shores touched by everything on all its other shores. There are plants in Italy seeded by winds from Egypt, and the farther west you move, the more of this cross-pollination you find. The Greek temple moved west and became a post office, a state capitol, and a railroad station. The Arabic house with its tile and filigree moved west and became Florida and California Spanish and eventually a motel.

So it was appropriate that our last stop was Spain, as it was the last stop for civilization in the Mediterranean. Everyone came here, the Phoenicians, the Greeks, the Romans with their aqueducts—which the Spaniards still drink from—Hannibal with his elephants lurching toward the Alps, various tribes from northern Europe, and the Arabs and Berbers from northern Africa whom the Spaniards called Moors.

In a building in Córdoba we found the summing up: an Arab caliph had it built as a mosque in Spain, by a Greek architect, and it is today being used as a Christian cathedral.

To try to get the facts as well as the feel and sound and flavor of this tumbling boil of human life on film and then on the air—while avoiding the cornball travelogue material about quaint native customs and the espionage of the trench coat and dangling cigarette—was what these travel programs were trying to do. I always loved exploring the ordinary, the everyday in the midst of journalism's preoccupation with great public events. The travel documentary, I found, was a very good vehicle for doing that, and for giving viewers a sense that news is not just about great leaders and great events, but also about the way ordinary people go about the business of life.

The Mississippi

Mark Twain got me interested in the Mississippi River. To him, it was not just a body of water, but a way of life—the crowded, busy, raffish artery that kept American commerce moving. Twain's *Life on the Mississippi* gave me the idea of taking my own trip down the river to see what it was like nearly a century after Twain described it. And in 1964, along with a very un–Twain-like retinue of producers and camera crews, I did it.

By then, life along the river was very different from that of Twain's time but not so different as to be unrecognizable. In fact, I suspect many parts of the Mississippi in 1964 were more like the Mississippi in 1864 than they were like the Mississippi of today. The great postwar expansion of the American economy had not yet reached a lot of the Midwest, which was still farming country and old industry. The term "urban renewal" had only recently entered the lexicon. There was no Gateway Arch at St. Louis, no Superdome in New Orleans. The federal interstate highway system had only begun to take shape there.

Up and down the Mississippi River and along its banks from Minnesota to Louisiana, I found living relics who seemed to personify the spirit of Mark Twain's characters: the grizzled frontiersman, the disheveled roustabout, the gruff, autocratic plantation boss, even a few surviving steamboat romantics. In 1964, the Chippewa Indians weren't the gambling kingpins they are today; they still pounded wild rice from stalks standing in the river's blue northern waters, just as they had for centuries. Roman Catholic nuns could be seen fishing from pontoons on their days off, habits awry, wielding cane poles and fancy casting rods. There was nothing extraordinary about river baptisms, their small bands of somber, plainly dressed people standing on the muddy banks singing hymns off-key. Abandoned shipyards and decaying steamboats littered the old industrial corridor between Iowa and Missouri.

In those days, segregated gangs of African American men still built the massive walls of protective revetments. And in the heart of the river's delta, one man farmed

30,000 acres of cotton in a town that bore his name, and local relations were more like those of an old European duchy than a democratic republic. Forty years ago, I caught a glimpse of this earthy world before it receded from view.

I think nearly every American has some notion about life along the Mississippi River, whether or not they've ever seen it, and I think we have Twain to thank for that. The name "Mark Twain" itself (the pen name for Samuel Langhorne Clemens) derived from Clemens's days on the river; it is a nautical term that means three fathoms, or eighteen feet. When Clemens was a boy before the Civil War in Hannibal, Missouri, he was smitten by his town's views of the "great Mississippi, the majestic, the magnificent Mississippi," which he likened to "a sort of sea, and withal a very still and brilliant and lonely one."

Clemens was by no means the only writer to fall in love with the Mississippi. Europeans visiting our young republic found the river just as mysterious—and also ominous, especially for its association with the slave trade. Charles Dickens and John James Audubon were horrified by the loud, coarse, sometimes violent passengers on the great steamboats. Harriet Martineau denounced the river as a highway of avarice and grief. Alexis de Tocqueville predicted in the 1830s that within fifty years, "the Mississippi valley will hold the mass of the American population." And New Orleans, he told his readers, "is certainly destined to be the largest city in the New World." Things didn't turn out quite that way, but the Mississippi's allure has never been tarnished; it has, in fact, inspired many of America's greatest artists. Think of Louis Armstrong or William Faulkner, W. C. Handy, Thomas Hart Benton, Richard Wright, Harriet Beecher Stowe, Jerome Kern, George Gershwin, and Paul Robeson—and then try thinking about them without thinking of the river.

The Mississippi is the longest river in the United States. Only the Nile is longer, and not by much. More impressive than its length is the Mississippi River's basin, which drains water from thirty-one states and two Canadian provinces, for a total of 1.24 million miles. Its several hundred tributaries create a navigable waterway system of more than 15,000 miles. Most people don't realize that the trunk of the Mississippi is formed by the intersection of three rivers: the Missouri, the Ohio, and the upper Mississippi. Ironically, the upper Mississippi is the least of these, but the seventeenth-century exploits of

Marquette, Joliet, and La Salle—all of whom stomped around the northern reaches of the river—ensured that the name "Mississippi" stuck. This was the place-name bestowed by the Ojibwa Indians of Wisconsin, meaning "Great River." The tribes of the lower valley memorialized the river's mighty flooding capacity by calling it "Father of Waters."

Some historians say that Columbus was the first white man to see the river, but Hernando de Soto generally gets credit for discovering it in 1541, somewhere within the boundaries of present-day Mississippi. Before Europe could take notice, though, he died and was buried beside it. A century passed before the French priest Marquette and his patron-explorer Joliet set out to map its course; they traveled as far south as the Arkansas delta before heading home to announce that it likely emptied into the Gulf of Mexico. La Salle came fast on their heels, believing the Mississippi might flow west into the Gulf of California—might provide the elusive shortcut to China. But, alas, he only confirmed that the river did indeed flow south. So La Salle planted what Clemens called a "confiscatory cross" somewhere in Arkansas, claimed the river and its land for Louis XIV (who promised him a monopoly on all buffalo hides therein), and named it Louisiana. When in 1803 Thomas Jefferson concluded negotiations with Napoleon Bonaparte and acquired the Louisiana Purchase, he knew almost nothing about what he had bought. That's why he sent Lewis and Clark on their famous journey of exploration.

The source of the Mississippi is Lake Itasca, in northern Minnesota. This cold northern end of the river is the least known—no steamboat, no riverboat gambler, no Mark Twain ever saw it, in part because it measures only ten feet wide and six inches deep. When I visited, families came out on Sundays to wade across, toting their babies in one hand, guiding their toddlers with the other. The area around Winona, Minnesota, was to me the prettiest part of the river, and it's there that I met Ralph Rickman, a self-proclaimed "river rat," which means he lived in, off, for, from, by, on, and near the river. Ralph had been a barge captain, but the vibrations from its diesel engines gave him indigestion, backaches, and sleepless nights. He quit when the company stopped serving its crew steak and strawberries for supper. When we met, Ralph lived with his teenage son George in a houseboat they had nailed together from an old North-western Railroad caboose and lumber from a Burlington Railroad passenger depot. Ralph grandiloquently dubbed it "a railroad merger." Crammed into this tight space were their meager belongings: a table, a stove, engine parts, fishnets, muskrat traps, three chairs, two bunks, hip boots, boat hooks, a heater, and oil lamps. That was it. There wasn't a whole lot of room inside, and when Ralph entered—at a strapping 250 pounds—the quarters got tighter still.

Ralph Rickman lived as close a life as I can imagine to what a grown Huck Finn would have chosen. He once went to Chicago, but didn't like it because he only saw an occasional dog. Ralph loved living close to nature, off the beaten path. He earned most of his money from the fish he sold to a wholesaler across the river in La Crosse, Wisconsin: carp, catfish, buffalos, and sheepheads. One of the more ingenious things he did for cash was to catch grasshoppers for catfish bait. Ralph took me out to a field to demonstrate how it was done. Mounting to the front of his car a plowlike "catcher"—which he made by welding two pieces of tin in the shape of a V, the top being a little longer than the bottom, and the back open—he drove around at a speed of between fifteen and twenty miles per hour, but only on days of at least sixty-five degrees; when lower, he said, the "hoppers won't hop." (Ralph advised that anyone trying this should "know your fields.") The grasshoppers were dumped from the catcher into a mesh bag, then transferred by hand into quart jars, which Ralph sold for a dollar each. His best year netted him $700. "Now that's a lot of hoppers," he chuckled.

When I headed south from Ralph's place, the river widened and the landscape changed dramatically, for it was there that the old industrial corridor running between Dubuque, Iowa, and St. Louis was located. These were the towns born of barges and steamboats, and the manufacturing and commerce they moved. In Dubuque I caught up with Richard Bissell, scion of an old, prominent family. Educated at Exeter and Harvard, he spent some years after college as a Mediterranean seaman before coming home to work as a Mississippi River pilot. Dick finally bent to family pressure and took over production at his great-grandfather's clothing factory, but he wasn't satisfied. In 1949, he won an *Atlantic Monthly* short-story contest, and the following year published his first novel, *A Stretch on the River.* For that, he won critical acclaim as Clemens's rightful heir. (Years later, Bissell responded playfully with another book subtitled *Why I Am Not Mark Twain*.) Bissell's biggest break came in the mid-1950s, when *7¹/₂ Cents*—a story of labor unrest at the Sleep-Tite pajama factory in an Iowa river town—was adapted for Broadway as *The Pajama Game*, and, later, as a Doris Day film. Dubuque was so proud of Dick the city fathers named a street for him, but it was not a splendid thoroughfare. Bissell Lane was three blocks long, had a few houses, a liquor store, five garages, and the back door to a dry-cleaning parlor. But its namesake had a soft spot for the used and unlovely, and he cherished this corner of his home town. "It's modest," he told me, "but we really love it, we love Bissell Lane. It's a bit of old Dubuque." Bissell went on: "Dubuque is not really a legend, it's a live town with 60,000 inhabitants, electricity, hot and cold running water, and Dubuque Star Beer is second to none in the Northwest Territories. Nowadays Dubuque is really bustling, bustling a bit too much for some of us old sentimental characters around here, especially when we see them tearing down a block of Victorian houses to make room for a parking lot or something like that. But Dubuque remains Dubuque, and the old-time flavor still remains."

Success did not faze Dick Bissell. He still liked boyish hijinks. He ran a towboat on the river, just for fun. Like Mark Twain, he revered the Mississippi; the smallest surviving trinket from its steamboat era was like gold to him. He amassed a tangle of riverboat antiques and memorabilia, which he kept in his brother's house and in a barn: ornate smoking stands, player pianos, blocks off old steamboats, a distress signal kit from 1913, periodical literature, concert posters, ticket stubs, Victrolas, a stuffed bird, Tiffany lamps—even the name board from the stern-wheel steamer *Aquila,* which he acquired *after* it sank. "We haven't taken an inventory here up in the barn for a good many years," Bissell joked, "but you just can't get that good inventory help anymore around here."

On Saturday nights, after depositing his and the other neighborhood children on a sandbar in the Mississippi, Dick liked to sit on his houseboat with friends and talk about the corn crop, boats, and, always, the river. Immersed as he was in its artifacts and history, Bissell simply glowed as he sat listening—not for the first time, I was sure—to his best friend recall their high school excursions on the steamer *Capitol,* which came upriver from St. Louis, its calliope audible from fifty miles out. "Do you remember how those engine rooms used to sound with those big reciprocating engines going back and forth?" Bissell asked, his eyes aglow.

"Well, you had a combination of two sounds, Dick," came the reply. "You had the paddle wheels kind of going flop, flop, flop, flop, flop, flop—like that—and then you had the steam exhausting out the chimneys, and that went [in a loud whisper], Ah! Wow! Haw! Whaa! Whoa! Yeah! . . ." And so went another evening on the Mississippi River all those years ago.

In 1964, the *Lone Star* was the last working classic steamboat left on the Mississippi River, and it made the most thoroughly pleasing noises, just as Dick Bissell's friend rendered them. The *Lone Star* was built in 1891; it carried no modern gadgets, no radar, no depth sounders, or any of that. Fired by hand, it moved gravel and sand, earned money, carried a pilot, two mates, an engineer, cook, and a Chihuahua dog that drank coffee. The *Lone Star* and hundreds like her came out of Kahlke's Boat Yard in Rock Island, Illinois; if the steamboat era was a Periclean golden age, Kahlke's was its Athens. When I visited, Kahlke's was little more than a steamboat cemetery of weeds, decay, and rust. Sitting on the hill there was the *W. J. Quinlan,* one of those wedding-cake steamboats, a shredding remnant of its former self. The *Quinlan* once traveled the river carrying a ten-piece band, six hundred people dancing in the ballroom, card games, and thirty-five-cent beer. When her owners went broke, others offered to buy the *Quinlan* and turn her into a floating restaurant, but old Fred Kahlke liked to look at her and so he refused to sell. By the time I arrived, the *Quinlan* was a rotting hulk of weathered timber, and Kahlke a wraith of an old man. He looked like an apparition from one of Mark Twain's novels, sitting there in his decrepit office, surrounded by piles of out-of-date calendars and un-opened mail. Everything looked as it had since its establishment in 1868—all, that is, except the buzz of customers ordering wooden steamboats. Kahlke was a wealthy man, a confirmed bachelor who wanted to leave his millions to the waitresses in a lo-cal bar. When we talked about his life and work, tears welled in his eyes, as his grav-elly voice intoned, "This place doesn't go too good. Wooden boats are about extinct.

Lots of sentiment is hooked into this Kahlke Boat Yard; it's been under the Kahlke name so long. We've had a meritorious reputation on the river. I hate to see the name go down but I'm getting to the age where I can't continue."

Kahlke rambled on: "The *Quinlan* was built in this yard in nineteen hundred and four. Yes, they were very nice trim-looking boats, we generally had a very nice design on the hull and plenty of shear in the boat, and railings along the upper decks, and cabins which always reminded me of a woman: to make 'em look nice, you had to dress 'em up. We miss the stern-wheel steamboats and the beautiful whistles they had. I could lay in bed and when a boat blew a-through the bridge, I'd know which one it was by the sound of its whistle. Now they all have air horns and you can't tell one from another."

A few miles downstream from Rock Island is Cairo, Illinois, where the Ohio River empties into the Mississippi. At one time the Gulf of Mexico extended clear up to Cairo, and over the ages the river's mud and silt piled up all or part of what is now Missouri, Kentucky, Tennessee, Arkansas, Mississippi, and Louisiana. This is some of the deepest, blackest, richest soil on earth—richer than the Nile delta—and it's cotton country. Cotton built an economy, a way of life, a way of doing business, and it built Memphis, where I watched the deft negotiations of cotton traders along Front Street. Memphis is the gateway to the Mississippi Delta, that corridor of antebellum splendor that extended to New Orleans before General Ulysses S. Grant and his Grand Army of the Republic arrived in 1862. This landscape also inspired the David O. Selznick image of the prewar South: giant live oaks draped in Spanish moss, miles of budding cotton plants, and massive Greek Revival plantation homes. Never mind that less than 1 percent of southerners ever lived that way; the wealth generated from cotton and sugar cane sustained these few in such opulence that it's not yet been forgotten.

Today, the summer of 1964 is remembered as "Freedom Summer," when busloads of young people from New York and other northern cities headed into Mississippi to register black voters and when some met a violent death at the hands of Klansmen and local police (who were sometimes the same people). My trip down the Mississippi River preceded theirs, but I too encountered the depths of southern racism—down in Plaquemines Parish, south of New Orleans. Leander

Perez, the long-time political boss of the parish (the Louisiana term for county), was ready for the civil rights movement. When I arrived, he showed me a cattle boat refitted with a wooden pen to hold people—specifically, he said, civil rights workers who entered Plaquemines or St. Bernard Parishes, the private preserves he'd dominated for nearly fifty years. Any demonstrators who showed up, he explained, would be herded down the river to a stockade, the site of an old Spanish fort, accessible only by boat or helicopter, or by wading through a swamp full of snakes. It was a remote and fierce place inhabited by mosquitoes so thick they could have choked a grazing cow. Back in the 1920s, Perez had been a close ally of Huey P. Long, when he was a populist governor. Perez served as Long's defense attorney at the governor's infamous impeachment trial in 1929, and for this act of loyalty, Long rewarded him with lucrative oil leases on state lands, which enriched Perez in short order. Perez ran his parishes like Huey Long ran the state, using oil revenues to provide roads and services. In private, Perez was called "Big Daddy." It wasn't uncommon for his slate to win elections by vote counts of 5,361 to 3, or even 0, and the list of registered voters in his parishes included the names of Babe Ruth, Herbert Hoover, Clara Bow, and Charlie Chaplin. "We plan ahead," he told me, with no hint of self-consciousness. In 1943, in the tradition of no-holds-barred Louisiana politics, then-governor Sam Jones attempted to rout Perez, literally, out of office. Perez's militia set up machine guns in the parish jail, and fled when state troops arrived. A ruling by the Louisiana State Supreme Court saved Perez by ruling the governor's actions unconstitutional. An outspoken segregationist, Perez created the Citizens' Council of Greater New Orleans in the 1950s, and helped found the Citizens' Council of America. He sponsored "Freedom Rides North" for any black person in Louisiana who wished to emigrate. As a result of his belligerent opposition to desegregation, Perez found himself excommunicated from the Catholic Church by Archbishop Joseph Francis Rummel.

Perez gave me a tour of his domain. We wound up sitting on a verandah late in the afternoon overlooking the Mississippi. I asked him whether he was a dictator. "People are jealous by nature," he shrugged. "We get along so well down here. We do so many things in parish government here that's not done elsewhere because they don't know how. They're jealous." Now wound up to talk, he continued expansively: "Our people are happy with employment; only half of one percent are unemployed. If we didn't have the threat and curse of bureaucracy upon us, and the awful federal government threatening us, we'd be happy people." Perez told me he had been pleased with his life's successes, but he feared the brewing civil rights movement, which he obliquely referred to as "the hopeless situation" in Washington and which he worried would undo his work. "You can't give up," he admonished me. "You can't feel frustrated, you have to keep playing along, have to help save our country and keep America great and keep our people happy. If only people could be as happy as those in Plaquemines Parish, we'd have no danger of communism, of infiltration, or anything approaching it, of bureaucracy. That bunch in Washington would be voted out so fast they'd be long since forgotten." At that moment Perez pulled a lighter out of his pocket, ready to stoke his signature cigar. Suddenly, a melody tinkled through the air. I asked, "What is that, a music-playing cigar lighter?" Perez, delighted by my question, said, "Yes, it plays 'Dixie,' don't you know that stirring song?" He laughed ominously and handed it to me. It had a Confederate flag burnished in its side.

In the many years since my trip down the Mississippi, various of my river hosts have passed away, and gambling casinos, whether on land or floating in garish boats, have sprouted up and down much of the river. In 1964, I concluded my trip believing that people on either end of the Mississippi would have little to say to one another; they don't understand each other, I thought, because they have nothing in common but the river. That is less true today. They all have gambling. The state of Mississippi is no longer the heart of darkness, but the nation's third most popular gaming destination. From New Orleans to the Chippewa Nation, one can find a Harrah's, a flamboyant stage show, and banquet tables loaded with food and alcohol. Once it was the steamboats that made the Mississippi a place of raffishness and debauchery. Now the casinos give people on both ends of the river plenty to talk about.

Two Cities on the Edge
of the Cold War

The Cold War did a lot of bad things to
the world. But to the countries that were
part of the great contest between capitalism and communism—the United States
and the Soviet Union most of all, but other
countries as well: Japan, Korea, most of
Western Europe, and others—the Cold
War was also a source of tremendous
energy. People worked harder, I always
thought, when they believed they were
part of a life-and-death competition. They
worked to make sure they were strong
enough to fight off the enemy, and they
worked to show the world that they were
doing better than their opponents.

But what about the places that were not
part of the competition, that were somehow on the sidelines of the Cold War, not
allowed to be part of the contest but not
able to escape from it either? I visited two
of those places, and made documentaries

about them, in the early 1960s, and they could not have been more different from each other. One of them was Vienna, the great capital of central Europe, seat of the Habsburg Empire, home of Beethoven and Mozart and Freud. The other was Hong Kong, a Chinese port city with nothing but commerce in its past, with no intellectual or artistic distinction. But these two very different cities, on opposite sides of the world, had one thing in common: they were on the edge of the Cold War, but not a part of it. Vienna, which bordered on the Soviet bloc in Eastern Europe, had become the capital of a neutral country in the 1950s when the Soviet occupying forces left, and it was careful to do nothing to antagonize the Kremlin after that. Hong Kong was the only piece of mainland China not under the control of the Communist government. Even though it was a British colony, it too had to keep its head down, to avoid being too hostile or too antagonistic toward Communist China. How these two places dealt with their marginal status in the Cold War was dramatically different.

In 1962, an Austrian citizen in his middle forties had lived through so much and most of it so bad, he felt he deserved a rest, and when I visited Vienna that year, he seemed to get plenty of it. Wire chairs set on the grass of the city's Stadtpark were usually filled on summer afternoons with people of all ages eating heavy pastry and listening to music. At that time, a typical forty-five-year-old Viennese had been born under the last emperor of what had been the Holy Roman Empire, and witnessed its collapse. If that wasn't enough, he had seen his country fight and lose both world wars. In between and after those momentous events, he had lived through a republic, a homegrown fascist dictatorship, a ruinous inflation, occupation by Hitler, and occupation by the Russians, and in 1955, by some miracle, he saw Austria get a peace treaty and its sovereignty. When I arrived in the summer of 1962, Austria was independent, socialist, neutral, overgoverned, underworked, overfed, and tired, a remnant of nineteenth-century Europe preserved in milk chocolate and whipped cream.

Sitting in those Stadtpark chairs, the Viennese seemed mesmerized by the strains of "The Emperor's Waltz," and Johann Strauss's other nostalgic compositions, as though they were beckoned by the past, and trying—with some success—to bring it back. The emperor of Strauss's waltz has long meant only one person to the Viennese: Franz Joseph of the great Habsburg line, emperor of Austria, king of Hungary, and heir to Charlemagne, who had founded the Holy Roman Empire in 800. Franz Joseph's royal robes are still on display, fresh and clean, looking as if he just shed them, and so is the dazzling crown of the Holy Roman Empire, representing a lineage that lasted a thousand years before dying in Vienna. It often occurred to me that the Viennese would like to see Franz Joseph in his royal garb again, to reassure them that, yes, they had indeed been a proud and sprawling empire of fifty-three million people, with a multiplicity of languages and cultures. To provide some perspective on the long shadow that Franz Joseph cast over his Middle European domain, consider that he sat on the throne—like a bump on a log—for sixty-eight years, from 1848 until he died in 1916, during the middle of World War I. In those same years, Americans lived under Presidents Polk, Taylor, Fillmore, Pierce, Buchanan, Lincoln, Andrew Johnson, Grant, Hayes, Garfield, Arthur, Cleveland, Benjamin Harrison, Cleveland again, McKinley, Theodore Roosevelt, Taft, and Wilson. The emperor's philosophy was simple: reign and change nothing. And except when forced to do so, he never did.

His only son, Crown Prince Rudolf, repeatedly urged his father to make reforms, to move Austria forward in those tumultuous last decades of the nineteenth century. For this Rudolf was ostracized as a dangerous radical and forced into an isolation that ended in tragedy one night at Mayerling, the royal hunting lodge outside Vienna. Rudolf, thirty years old, went there one night with Mary Vetsera, a lady friend; the next morning their bodies were found, the victims of a double suicide. When the emperor heard of his son's fate, he allegedly broke down, perhaps for the only time in his long life. One account captures his bitterness, which echoed in his pronouncement "He died like a tailor!" Naturally, the Habsburg family found the scandal intolerable, so they ordered Mary Vetsera's body spirited away and buried in a quiet country cemetery. Rudolf was publicly laid to rest in the royal Habsburg vaults, but his family refused to acknowledge what had occurred. Gossip ran on for years across Europe; it stopped eventually, but the plays, movies, television programs, and books—several dozen, in fact—still continue. A lot of this has been soap opera rubbish, and no doubt entertaining, but the point is that had Rudolf lived and been listened to, Austria might have entered the twentieth century peacefully, and without bringing on the First World War, whose consequences we still live with. In short, the only brain in the Habsburg family able to understand that the world was changing was Rudolf's, and he put a bullet through it.

I found the Viennese painfully aware of this romantic, fairy-tale past. They lived in an exquisite imperial city built on a majestic scale, reduced to governing a country smaller than Mississippi. During the Cold War, Austria constituted the eastern boundary of non-Communist Europe, bordered on the east and the south by Hungary and the former states of Czechoslovakia and Yugoslavia. It was decidedly eastern and Balkan in temperament and pace, betrayed only by a western-style devotion to the internal combustion engine, preferably in a car but if not, in a motor scooter, accessorized with a pretty girl perched daintily on the back.

The really serious business in Vienna was eating—as many as six times a day. A visiting American concerned about his weight was viewed somewhat suspiciously since the Viennese believed, as did Samuel Johnson, that anyone who didn't mind his belly would hardly mind anything else. There are many excellent Viennese dishes, but the city is renowned for its pastries, so luscious and lavish they make their French equivalents look dainty. Whether at a sidewalk *würstchen* stand or in the most elegant of dark-paneled restaurants (where the service is quite possibly the best in the world), gastronomy is relished in Vienna. I remember dropping by the kitchen at the famed Hotel Sacher one afternoon, to watch the staff prepare a tray of appetizers for a room service call, a "little something" for a guest languishing in his room with those light hunger pangs that descend between lunch and dinner. This "little something" nearly overwhelmed a large silver tray—a veritable banquet of fruits, cheeses, cold fish, and pastry. In spite of myself, I found the Viennese devotion to gastronomic excess quite charming. Sacher's is proudest of its pastries, and when I was there, the hotel let the public know as much, as an American establishment of the same era boasted of its air conditioning and its swimming pool.

Café Demel was Vienna's most famous pastry shop and Sacher's foremost competitor, everything in its overstuffed showcases was hand-made fresh every day. This was where hundreds of Viennese came each morning, between breakfast and lunch, after lunch, after dinner, and after the opera for a little coffee *mit schlag,* and a little pastry *mit schlag.* In 1962, the Viennese were fiercely advocating one side or the other of an imbroglio precipitated by the two establishments' competing claims to the original Sacher torte recipe.

There are varieties and subvarieties of pastries in Vienna, but without question, the Sacher torte, or cake, is the most highly regarded, not least for its pedigreed origins. Back in 1814, after Napoleon's defeat and exile, Austria's scheming foreign minister, Prince Metternich, called together the Congress of Vienna—a convention, so to speak, of Europe's kings and princes. It took nine months for the congress to redraw the map of Napoleon's empire. Metternich, determined to hold sway over his royal visitors, commissioned Harry Sacher to create a new and heavy pastry, with which Metternich could subdue his opposition. Armed with this confection of cake, marmalade, and chocolate—the Sacher torte—Metternich kept his guests' stomachs full enough and their minds drowsy enough to craft an agreement that kept Europe at relative peace until 1914. And every day since, the Sacher torte has been prepared and served in Vienna. For this reason, it is considered a national treasure, at least as worthy as the crown jewels, and certainly more nourishing.

I arrived in Vienna in the middle of a legal wrangle, which in 1962 had already been six or seven years in the making. The issue, which Viennese courts were trying to settle, concerned basic questions of justice and honor: did the Café Demel torte, with its triangular seal, or the Hotel Sarcher torte, with its round seal, have the right to advertise its dessert as the original Sacher torte? I interviewed the publisher of a cultural monthly, who tried to impress upon me the gravity of the question: "Of course you must realize, that which is the true Sacher torte belongs very much in the realm of culture in Austria; the Viennese really do care about these things, it's one of the very few things they really care about." The trouble started in 1931 or thereabouts, when the proprietor of the Hotel Sacher, built sometime in the 1880s, died. Edward Sacher, the grandson of the man who did Metternich's bidding and invented the torte, took the recipe and sold it to Demel, and ever since, Café Demel has felt justified to manufacture and sell the original Sacher torte. After World War II, however, the Hotel Sacher reopened under new management—not related to the original family—and they thought it would be a grand idea to bring back the Sacher torte. So they improvised a little, adding a second layer of marmalade to the cake. My publisher friend called this layer "extremely unorthodox and detested by all true connoisseurs of the Sacher torte." Well, Café Demel sued the Hotel Sacher to force it to refrain from calling its torte by the same name.

I don't now recall how the suit was resolved—long after my visit. But today, the Sacher torte is a major Austrian export, and the Hotel Sacher, by hook or by crook, is once again the only establishment daring to claim it has the original recipe.

As this story suggests, the Viennese were somewhat overfed, and in 1962, they were also underworked, which meant that they were a hefty people. This condition could be seen in its most extreme form on construction jobs where laborers—who in other places are often lean and muscular—spent long, lovely, lazy days standing around, mostly. We recorded evidence of this fact with a hidden camera, and in myriad locations throughout the city. It became comical to us, this lack of activity at heavy-construction sites, and reinforced the punch line of a joke then making the rounds: the Viennese liked to say that their country's recovery from the devastation of World War II was the greater miracle when compared to Germany's, since the Germans worked for theirs. In part, I think the lassitude grew from an old Viennese tradition of looking at work long and carefully before actually doing any. But at lunchtime, these men suddenly came to life when, at the appointed time, one of their fellows went out for beer and everybody *really* stopped working. To quit something you haven't begun is quite an undertaking, and these men were skilled at it. The storekeepers behaved similarly; they closed up at the slightest provocation, and went home for several hours at midday to eat and nap. All businesses closed their doors on Saturday afternoons, Sundays, legal holidays, religious holidays, national holidays, and all other special days, as they were decreed. It is said that Empress Maria Theresa once resorted to importing some hardworking people from Czechoslovakia to set an example for the Viennese, but it did not help: they soon quit working too.

On their days of respite from the brutal daily grind, the Viennese liked to leave the city center by the thousands, to head for the Vienna Woods, the legendary park on the edge of town celebrated by Strauss's "Tales from the Vienna Woods." There, with rucksacks, heavy shoes, and often in lederhosen, they hiked, climbed hills, and, of course, ate heartily from their weighty picnic baskets. For these and other reasons, the Austrians are often described as Germans with a southern drawl, slower in speaking and slower in working. The furious work habits of the Germans, I was told, led to heart attacks, nervous ailments, ulcers, and a tightness across the stomach, which the Viennese called "manager's sickness." They rejoiced that their culture was not so afflicted. In turn, there seemed to be little sense of competition between Austrians. If one man made more money than his neighbor, it wasn't perceived as a reflection of higher intelligence or a superior work ethic, but that he was greedy, and possibly a thief.

To the outside world, Vienna is synonymous with Baroque architecture, and there is a good reason why: the city is home to the world's largest collection of these ornate, monumental buildings. During the eighteenth century, as a reaction to the severe architectural style of the Protestant Reformation and in an effort to celebrate the splendor of the Habsburg monarchy, the Viennese went for the Baroque with abandon, building the magnificent Ringstrasse in the heart of the city, lined with parks, massive stone buildings, and heroic monuments; the Schönbrunn and Belvedere Palaces; and elaborate garden ruins, designed to look like crumbling Roman relics the day they were finished. Probably the most magnificent Baroque building in all Vienna is the national library, designed by Fischer von Erlach as the private preserve of the Habsburg family. You might call it a cathedral of books of overwhelming splendor, perhaps the most magnificent library in the world, built for a family that never cared much for reading.

The University of Vienna was a thriving intellectual center in the fourteenth century—even before Christopher Columbus was born—and until the early 1930s was a center for scholarship and discovery, particularly in medicine. Sigmund Freud is just one name on a long list of giants who worked there. When I visited, the greatest of its minds had long since departed. In 1933, Austria's homegrown fascist government combed through the list of faculty and fired those suspected of ever having held a liberal or progressive opinion. The Nazis came five years later and dismissed first the Jews and then the Catholics. When the war was over, the Austrians took up the job again and fired the people the Germans had installed. No campus can survive purges like that, and this one did not. By the early 1960s, it seemed as though the only professors were those who never in their lives had offended anybody, on the right or the left. The good ones had gone to the United States or Britain and refused to come back. In 1962, even the buildings were falling apart. A deeply conservative institution, the university found no favor with the socialist bureaucracy of Vienna, which refused to give it even enough money to paint the ceilings. Vienna in its prewar and postwar misery suffered a great deal, but the destruction of the university may have been its greatest loss of all.

With Hitler gone and the Russians gone, the Austrians built a labyrinthine bureaucracy to govern themselves, and its badge of honor was the briefcase. In the early 1960s, a civil servant on the street without one was not fully dressed. Many satchels held no briefs or papers at all, but cold beef sandwiches, cheese, bread, and garlic sausage. In the offices at 10 a.m., a flurry would begin when the briefcases were unsnapped and everybody ate to stave off the long and agonizing two-hour wait for lunch.

Those who were not deskbound during

the morning or any other time found their
way to a Vienna institution justly and
widely celebrated: the coffeehouse. Its origins went back three centuries to the Siege
of Vienna, when, after a successful rout
of the Turks, some enterprising person
opened an establishment with coffee beans
left behind by the enemy. The city's other
contributions to civilization include the
operetta, Mozart, Beethoven, Schubert,
Sigmund Freud and psychoanalysis, the
Sacher torte, leather pants, boiled beef, and
a talent for enjoying life, which ought to
be enough. But the coffeehouse was (and
may still be) a place where people could go
and sit as long they liked, buy as little as
they liked or nothing at all, be handed the
newspapers one by one, one glass of water
after another, coffee and pastry if they
wanted it. They could have coffee plain,
half milk, cold, hot, with ginger, with
brandy, *mit schlag,* or any other way. If a
customer brought in a dog, he was welcome too, and was provided a special mat
to sit on, as other places provide high
chairs to children. No customer was urged
to order anything; nobody was brought a
check until it was requested. The coffeehouse was a club, a retreat, a place for tired
feet and empty stomachs, an altogether
splendid and civilized institution. If anyone

in Vienna ever did contract a case of manager's sickness, this would have been the place to cure it.

I spoke with Fritz Weiss, a local man-about-town, who reminisced with me about the Viennese art of living, and how it had changed since the war. "We eat well, we drink well, we enjoy our food, the Viennese are for all of that," he began. "We hear music, we like the arts, that's what is called living well. What I like most about the Viennese, though, is that they do not know a final 'no,' they may give you a 'no,' and you may even oppose it and get another 'no,' but it's never a final no." All that said, Weiss lamented the passing of a halcyon prewar era. People were no longer open and friendly, he said, because during the Nazi occupation, neighbors and acquaintances could not know who might be an informant. "Therefore people withdrew more to family life, to the closest family, and even the closest family was sometimes not safe enough," he told me sadly. "Austria once contributed a lot to the culture of the world, and it is natural to be reminded of that when walking through the streets," he said, making note of the places Beethoven, Schubert, and Mozart lived and worked. "We think it is nice."

Houses once occupied by Beethoven are all over town. The great composer began losing his hearing in early life, and banged his piano so loudly that his neighbors always hounded him to move. The figures vary, but it's estimated that he lived in about thirty different places in as many years. Today, of course, Austrians hold him in high honor, in a country that, more than any other, devotes time, money, and effort to music. In Vienna, it is never lacking. Take the city's famed opera house, for instance, the site of performances conducted by Verdi and Wagner. Gustav Mahler was once installed there as its artistic director. On opera days, I saw lines of Viennese waiting to buy tickets—to seats, if they could afford them, or to standing room, if they could not. It wasn't uncommon for the standees to pay the equivalent of less than a dollar to get in, and then to be on their feet for more than six hours.

As the State Opera, it was owned and subsidized by the Austrian government at a lavish rate, in 1962 anyway. Government ownership and subsidy produced some nasty tempests: if an orchestra conductor didn't care for a particular horn player, or if a choreographer complained about an overweight, flat-footed ballerina, there was little that could be done, since the artists were civil service employees and immune from firing. The rules governing the work regimen and hours of the opera-house stagehands were similarly rigid; it wasn't uncommon for the theater's heavy asbestos curtain to come down before the singers had finished their bows. Despite these nettlesome details, the musical standards of the State Opera House were, and remain, extremely high. The audiences are demanding and critical, but they can also be warmly sentimental. Favorite singers who are well past their prime are applauded not so much for how they sound on a given night, but for how they used to sound.

There is an evocative story about the construction of the opera house, which took roughly eight years to build during the 1860s, while Americans were fighting the Civil War. The opera house was purported to be a model of the early French Renaissance style, but in fact it turned out to be a rather eclectic assortment of pinnacles, colonnades, and monumental statuary. Emperor Franz Joseph announced that he didn't care for it, so the architect who designed it committed suicide. In several other cases, Viennese architects whose buildings displeased their clients also killed themselves, a practice, thankfully, that has never caught on among their American colleagues. The opera house still bears a sullen association with Hitler, who, as a young bum living in Vienna, saw hundreds of performances of Wagner's operas there. During World War II, an American bomber pilot mistook the building for the city's railroad station and bombed it, destroying everything but the front entrance. It was rebuilt by 1955—ahead of schools or hospitals—and financed in part by funds from the Marshall Plan.

Speaking of World War II and Vienna, a surreal and little-known battle occurred there in 1945 in the Prader, a late-nineteenth-century amusement park fifteen minutes from the city center. When the Russians entered Vienna on their advance toward Germany, a grotesque and dreamlike battle was fought here. To appreciate the surreal nature of this story, I should explain that the Prader is one of those intact old amusement parks, all wooden and hand-painted. Imagine the incongruity of machine guns and rifle fire through the merry-go-round, and mortar and hand grenades exploding around the Ferris wheel. A group of German soldiers caught in the fun house were so confused by the distorting mirrors they couldn't find their way out, and were killed inside. This may have helped inspire the postwar film

The Third Man, with Orson Welles, much of which also took place in the Prader.

There were in the Vienna of 1962 these stark and melancholy ghosts of Hitler's *Anschluss,* and a keen awareness of paradise lost. The Viennese were so much in love with their past they refused to leave it. Many of them told me they reckoned their country to be two generations behind Western Europe, but that was just fine by them. They did as little work as possible, enjoying instead their rich food and beverages, preferably with whipped cream; they frequented the opera, the coffeehouses, the pastry shops, the parks, the Prader, and the Vienna Woods. They enjoyed art only if it depicted a tree, a flower, a waterfall, or a jowly duke wearing a red uniform. They took warm pride in their city's affinity for operettas played out on a stage full of red velvet, crystal chandeliers, and curving stairways. It seemed to me that all of Vienna was a stage. I half expected each day to see the Prince of Belgravia come around the corner to proclaim, slightly off-key, his undying love for the overweight soprano.

Not long before we went to Vienna, we traveled to Hong Kong for another installment of the "Our Man in . . ." series. To westerners, the Mediterranean is the cradle of civilization, but to Asians it's China. Hong Kong was then and still is a combination of both—Chinese and European. But since 1949, it has had the distinction of being a bastion of capitalism in the shadow of the world's most populous Communist country. And unlike Vienna, which dealt with the colossus to its east by hunkering down, somewhat sleepily, into a dream of its past, Hong Kong dealt with the colossus to its north by exhibiting an almost incredible energy.

After a thirty-hour flight from the United States, we climbed off the airplane in Hong Kong red-eyed, rumpled, sleepy, squinting in the sun, our left arms still sore from smallpox and typhoid shots. Hong Kong was still a British crown colony, still hanging on as a tiny dot of capitalism on the vast mainland of Communist China, almost forty years before it would revert back to Chinese control—something no one at the time seemed to believe would ever happen; if they did, they considered it so far in the future as to not be worth worrying about. When we were there, the colony had recently acquired a notoriety as a place seething with intrigue, reeking of opium, crawling with smugglers, a place where spies slipped secrets across the Red Chinese border concealed inside live pigs. There was some truth to all of this, and Hong Kong therefore had become a setting for bad novels and assorted movies and television series.

We spent three weeks there shooting a film, not trying to photograph the spies or the opium smugglers, who were not easy to catch in good light anyway, but attempting to see how it was for the millions of Chinese who had fled from Communism and for the British who ran the colony and furnished them with a place to flee to. We found that these refugees were so numerous, so anxious to work, and paid so little that labor was Hong Kong's cheapest commodity, and handmade goods sold at prices that ranged from low to absurdly low. A man's suit, hand-tailored of English woolen, was $40, an incredible price even in 1961. At the end of a day of work, our film crew members put down their cameras, lights, and film spools, and melted into the shadows of the tailors' fitting booths. There was a closed-circuit, wired television system run by the British, and about a third of the programs were American. I was in a booth being fitted when the Chinese tailor asked where I worked. I said, "For television in the United States."

He said, "Oh, yes. *Highway Patrol. Wagon Train.* You want two pants?" A half dozen American military planes flew in one day and parked on one side at the airport. I asked somebody why they were there. He said, "Oh, that's the U.S. Navy. They're in here buying suits."

The colony was so crowded that many people who couldn't find a house or an apartment lived on the water. Large areas of the harbor were jammed with junks and sampans and rafts, on which families who couldn't find (or didn't want) a place to stay on shore lived all year round. The floating neighborhood of the harbor was itself like a city. You could be born, grow up, go to some kind of school, buy your clothes and food, have your teeth fixed, get married, have children, grow old, and die all without ever setting foot on land. On the harbor, people didn't go to the stores. The stores came to them, in the form of small, fast-moving boats carrying food and clothing and other goods moving from place to place, looking for customers.

Other refugees slept on the sidewalks. An entire Chinese family would pile up a pitiful little shelter of cardboard and flattened tin cans against the side of a building, and then live in it. The British authorities tolerated this as far as they could, while trying to build sturdier housing fast enough to keep the sidewalks clear. But it was not fast enough, because the refugees still slipped past the police at the Communist border and got into the colony at the rate of about a thousand a week. Somehow they kept alive, and most of them found some little jobs with tiny incomes and then worked aggressively toward something better. The British colonial governor of Hong Kong told me, "If you help a Chinese once, that's all he wants. The next time you'll see him is when he drives around in his new car to thank you."

The colony that was created by this Chinese energy and aggressiveness was, to me, the most exciting place in the world. The pace was faster than New York's. The Chinese squeezed and pushed down the narrow streets like water through a pipe. For about eighteen hours a day, there was what in America would pass for rush hour. The result was a fantasy of odd noises, flashing colors, families living on sidewalks, boats, rooftops, hillsides, working or looking for work, smoking opium, gambling, celebrating with firecrackers some occasion large or small, carrying babies in slings on their backs, haggling in the stores over prices that were already too low.

Beyond the city, in the mountainous land

this side of the Communist border, you could find twenty miles of ancient Chinese farmland, looking just as it did two thousand years ago—with men and women, barefoot, standing in muddy water to their knees, wearing peaked straw hats and working in rice paddies, looking like a classic Oriental print done in thin lines and pale colors. But in Hong Kong itself, everything was changing almost as fast as the blink of an eye—a city flooded with new people, new buildings, new businesses, and new energy roaring into the future with hardly a thought to the past. There was no place like it in the world. It was as far as could be from sleepy Vienna's Old World languor and pastry-laden cafés, even though it too was shaped to a large degree by being in the shadow of the Cold War.

Three Beaches

During the heady, speculative days of the early twentieth century, Henry Flagler, an enterprising oil and railroad magnate, cleared the dense scrubby foliage of south Florida, built the Florida East Coast Railway all the way to Miami, and created a resort paradise for wealthy northerners. The crash of 1929 changed all that, and pretty dramatically. After World War II Florida recovered, and its growth ever since has outstripped most of the nation's.

Not until the early 1960s, however, did this spectacular growth reach the little town of Cocoa Beach—near Cape Canaveral on the Atlantic Coast, a short drive from Orlando. Only a few years earlier, Cocoa Beach had consisted of little more than a wooden shack selling fishing bait and sandwiches; there was no real money to be found there, just a few people, and an abundance of snakes. But the

Department of Defense had been at Cape
Canaveral since 1948, directing missile and
satellite launches—fairly quietly until the
Russians announced their successful orbit
of a satellite in 1957. At that point, Congress got to work and passed the National
Aeronautics and Space Act, creating
NASA. To the few old-timers there, the
place quickly became unrecognizable: in
almost no time, Cocoa Beach found itself
rich, full of traffic jams, and crowded with
all kinds of people.

At one point when I was in Florida covering one of the space launches, I decided
it would be interesting to look at the effects of the spectacularly popular space
program on the little town that was now
identified with it. So I rented a baby blue
convertible and drove out on the hard-
packed white sand to take a casual inventory of the beachcombers. I found groups
of beatnik party-folk lazing around, drinking beer and dancing the limbo; I saw
young mothers, the wives, probably, of
Cape Canaveral engineers, building sand
castles with their children; I even eaves-
dropped on a convention of young Pres-
byterian boys from some other part of the
country, there to contemplate the implica-
tions of space exploration for their Christian faith.

All this activity at Cape Canaveral, spurred even further by President Kennedy's commitment to a manned space flight to the moon, created opportunity for Jake Brodsky, a retired Air Force sergeant, who saw that lots of money could be made. With seemingly little effort, he built an empire of bowling alleys, beer stands, motels, and nightclubs to serve off-duty missile men and their families. Brodsky was a large, amiable, middle-aged man who liked Hawaiian shirts. When I caught up with him poolside at one of his motels, he was asking two young women in bathing suits if they had liked the previous night's floor show and inviting them to take a swim. For our interview on camera, he stepped out of his usual attire and settled on a pressed string tie, reminding me of Colonel Sanders. I asked him to give me the history of his tropical empire.

"I think," he said, "it's like the general who got there first with the most. We started with the bowling alley, then opened up a little grocery store, and before I knew it, I had a seven-day work schedule. Let's see, the office buildings came next, then the Vanguard Motel, the Mayfair Cafeteria, and yes, the offices for Martin Marietta." From a bowling alley to office towers, so went Cocoa Beach, and much of south Florida.

I also checked in with a real estate agent, another symbol of the transformed landscape. She was an overweight woman with bleached hair, weathered face, huge white sunglasses, and pink lipstick, and she represented a large tract of scrub palmettos dubiously called "Canaveral Groves Estates." Like Jake Brodsky, this woman was imbued with the possibility of getting rich, and quickly. She tried to tempt me with an offer of an acre of tangled scrub, a few hundred feet from the sparkling beach, for only $1,599—which I could finance for ten dollars down and fifteen a month. We stood on top of a tower while she made her pitch, overlooking the brush below. I'll never forget her disingenuous reply to my question, "How about the snakes?" Without skipping a beat, she said, with authority, "This may be virgin land, Mr. Brinkley, but I haven't encountered any. I've never even been bitten by a mosquito here."

While the jazzy and the new were booming in Cocoa Beach, the old and the quiet were left to die. The Cocoa Hotel, built in 1883, was a pleasing white clapboard establishment set in a grove of magnolia and palmetto with wide porches and tall ceilings. Sitting in rocking chairs out front, I found its two elderly proprietors, a pair of sisters born and raised there. I asked them how business had been since the space program had taken off. "Business is not so good," said the tougher of the two. "It's like me, it's gotten aged." The sisters told me that the so-called business section of Cocoa Beach had, for almost their entire long lives, been a mere two blocks long. Like most rural southern crossroads, that meant a feed and seed store and a gas station. People had always kept their own cattle, pigs, and chickens, and lots of them subsisted on fish, which they got up and caught every day. Beyond these two sandy blocks of old Cocoa, all around, lay the dense Florida woods. "I don't like what's going on here," my gruff informant told me, with more than a glimmer of indignation in her old eyes.

I found it hard to disagree with her. Over at the boomerang-style Polaris Motel, its neon lights blinking wildly, I met Miss Peggy Lloyd, a buxom, platinum-blond lounge singer, whose trademark tune went something like "He's locked up in that capsule, he can't get away. When I call up to Canaveral, everything's A-OK, A-OK." Miss Lloyd's jokes weren't much better. Night after night, she spoofed, "Welcome to Cuckoo Beach! Well, this is the space age—two years behind the Russians, and ten years behind the comic books!" The nightly crowd at the Polaris consisted of young professional men and their wives, the mothers and fathers of the baby boom generation, laughing, smoking, drinking highballs and martinis—in short, feeling on top of the world.

On launch days an unrivaled excitement and seriousness of purpose gripped everyone. Crowds filled the dunes, clutching binoculars; high school science clubs hauled their homemade tracking equipment out onto the beach. People of all ages and backgrounds set up telescopes and those heavy reel-to-reel tape recorders, to capture a remarkable piece of history. Meanwhile, Jake Brodsky, back at the Vanguard Motel, busily ordered his staff about: "Set up for five to six hundred people around the pool. We're going to have a real starlight celebration, a real party tonight."

If postwar Florida is synonymous with the space program, it is also synonymous with the growth of another American industry: the motel. The traditional pattern for an industry, as for an individual, is to start in humble style—preferably in a log cabin—and through energy and initiative to rise to prominence and prosperity. Well, the story of the American motel is not one that began *in* a log cabin, but *as* a log cabin. The legend is that the first motel appeared in Kansas in 1848, a place where covered wagons could pull off the Santa Fe Trail and stop for the night. In two years it sold $200,000 worth of food and rifles, $14,000 worth of whiskey, and $12 worth of Bibles.

Eighty years later, in the late 1920s, little square boxes began sprouting at the back of roadside gas stations. They were called tourist cabins. It ran about a dollar to spend a night, or maybe an hour or so, and the "cabins" acquired a shady reputation. After the war, "mom-and-pop" operations cropped up, modest stucco row structures built with the life savings of a retired couple. Often, late at night, when the last room was rented, mom would come out in her bathrobe, collect six or eight dollars, and hang the NO VACANCY sign in the window.

By the early 1960s in Miami Beach, a visitor from that period would be boggled and a little bewildered to see what was, at the time, the ultimate development of the motel architectural form: a motel called the Castaways. There was no gimmick it did not have. For lack of a better term, the style might be called "tiki," or "Miami Beach Polynesian." Joe Hart, who had previously run a restaurant chain called The Pickin' Chicken, borrowed almost $2 million from the Teamsters Union to build the Castaways; he designed it himself and had to argue with the architect to get him to build parts of it—and it showed.

The motel's 304 rooms catered to 30,000 guests annually for a mere $16.50 per night. For this, patrons might enjoy a Shinto temple dining room with a parabolic roof, grass shacks built by Seminole Indians, and a public address system operated by a woman with a nasal Brooklyn accent, repeating ad nauseam all day long things like "Ladies and gentlemen, your attention please. Tonight is Rebel Night at the Castaways, featuring a delicious dinner of southern fried chicken," and "Ladies and gentlemen, the Castaways Wreck Bar is now open for your pleasure. Visit the Wreck Bar for your favorite cocktails, and watch our underwater swimmers." On any given day, the scene poolside looked like something from a B movie: thirty- and forty-year-olds, a little overweight, dancing the Twist to the strains of a live band, drinking oversized cocktails adorned with colorful umbrella swizzle sticks.

When I caught up with Joe Hart, the Castaways's proprietor, he sat a short distance from the pool wearing a pressed cotton suit, his eyes hidden behind a large pair of black sunglasses. His secretary, matronly and prim, sat beside him, taking dictation. With an air of self-importance, Hart told me, "The motel of today is really a far cry from what we knew as a motel just a few years ago. We actually have to think for our guests because they come here and just want to relax. We have child counselors who supervise the children while their parents can frolic around. We have two bands, we have wonderful shows—in fact, we have a different shindig here every night. I would say that every night of the week is New Year's Eve at the Castaways. We have nicknamed our place 'America's Most Funderful Resort Motel.' "

So from a log cabin beside the Santa Fe Trail, we had arrived, in the early 1960s, at the Castaways, a roadside spectacular. If the motel art form had developed any further, we might not have wanted to look at it. From a place selling beds, food, rifles, whiskey, and Bibles evolved the Castaways and its formidable list of services: five pools, baby-sitters, lollipop hunts, a beauty salon, all-night dancing, washers and dryers, free movies, Swedish massage, and a solarium for sunbathing stark naked. Now that's what I call progress.

In the early sixties, Cocoa Beach and Miami Beach were in what might be called their primes. Several thousand miles away, I visited another beach that had passed its prime. Brighton, on the southeastern coast of England, was nineteenth-century Britain's equivalent of Miami Beach. Unlike American resorts, though, the surf at Brighton is nearly always too cold to swim in, and people sunbathe in felt hats and overcoats. Two centuries before my visit, a British physician named Richard Russell published a book about the medical benefits of seawater. Russell maintained that bathing in it and drinking it would cure gland ailments, headaches, and vertigo; it would strengthen the brain and nervous system, and banish melancholia. Believe it or not, bathing in and swallowing ocean water became a huge fad in eighteenth-century England, and the nearest place that Londoners could take the cure was at Brighton, then just a small fishing village.

Nobody drinks seawater any longer, but

Londoners in the early 1960s still poured out of their flats on holiday to grab a train for Brighton, including a high-speed express called the Brighton Belle, which took about an hour door-to-door. Roaring in from London in a cloud of dust and flying candy wrappers, my fellow passengers and I headed straight for the beach wearing heavy coats, because even on the southernmost coast of England, it's often chilly, even occasionally in August.

In the early nineteenth century, the Prince of Wales, who became King George IV, made Brighton a center of high fashion and society with his Royal Pavilion, a dazzling palace designed by the famed British architect John Nash, who fancifully combined Indian Mughal architecture with Chinese interiors. The Pavilion was long associated with Prince George's sumptuous parties, his gambling and romantic trysts; the goings-on at Brighton kept English society perpetually titillated. And for that reason, music hall comedians still refer to Brighton with a leer, and can elicit robust laughter, even though it's long been a perfectly respectable place. George IV was a great patron of the arts and architecture, leaving behind the restored Windsor Castle, and the newly constructed Buckingham Palace in London. Remaining in Brighton from his time are many handsome Regency houses, once occupied by London intellectuals who commuted to their posts in the city. But by the early 1960s, Brighton was mainly a working-class resort, a place to spend a weekend or a Sunday, to sit in the thin chilly sun, bring a picnic lunch, and for all but the young and the brave, to stay away from the cold ocean water.

What I remember of Brighton is the crowds of weatherbeaten, middle-aged working people who, for a few pennies, rented comfortable canvas chairs, and promptly fell asleep. They seemed worn still by the calamities of both world wars: to pass a cool and soothing afternoon listening to the surf, to the shouts of ice cream vendors and children, seemed all they could muster energy for. It was amusing to walk along the water's edge, and to hear from one end of the beach to the other the same BBC soap opera on hundreds of battery radios. This particular day I remember the melodramatic attempts of a man named Gerald to persuade his lover, Brenda, to tell her husband, Henry, about their affair. Finally, after the episode concluded, and that intense period of emotional strain and excitement had subsided, the Brighton beachcombers sat up and took out their lunches: sandwiches, cheese, fruit, ice cream. One generalization I can comfortably make about the British in those days is that they were always prepared to eat, no matter what went on around them.

The placidness that enveloped Brighton was a pleasure—and a far cry from the contrived gaiety of Cocoa Beach and the Castaways. I asked a few people if they'd change anything, given the chance, but most of the answers were given in such heavy Cockney accents, it was difficult to grasp their complete replies. What I did learn is that some folks thought the price of the deck chairs a bit too high; others complained of the beatniks who had started showing up; and others thought generally that people had changed for the worse since 1945. It wasn't until late afternoon, when the sun was low and it was too cold even to sit and look at the water, that people began to shuffle away. This is when the beach becomes visible, or, more accurately, the rocks. Far and away, what people complained most about was the lack of space and comfort by the water. They wanted sand, the kind we have along our Atlantic coast. Once the chairs were largely vacated, an idler or two could be seen stepping among them, looking to see whether someone had left anything of interest or value behind: a piece of jewelry perhaps, or a coin. Even though it was cold, the peace at Brighton in the late afternoon was alluring.

I took leave of the shoreline to explore Brighton's quiet lanes, a remnant of its Regency days, filled with a charming array of stores, antiques, books, and George Alexander, a wandering harpist who had been playing his tinkling instrument in those streets for sixty-six years. There was a fitting mournfulness to his music, like a ghost from Brighton's past.

I spent my late afternoon visiting King George IV's Pavilion, which must be one of the most hideously fascinating buildings in the world. He built a modest royal retreat there in 1788, but years later, after someone sent him some Chinese wallpaper, George IV ordered the entire thing rebuilt to match its pattern. The result, in my opinion, is a bad dream of Indo-Chinese, Moorish curry–flavored gingerbread, inside and out. For George IV, it was a pleasure dome, a place for licentious episodes in a day when causing a scandal took some doing. It was kept as a museum, and I had the pleasure of touring it with its curator, the impeccable Clifford Musgrave. The British can wax so eloquently about the most pedestrian things, and Mr. Musgrave's peroration on the expansive chandelier hanging in the dining room was no exception. "I suppose," he said, "that it's the most famous thing here. It hangs from a domed ceiling that's painted like a spreading palm tree, and then just below the leaves of the palm tree is an enormous dragon carved out of wood and covered with burnished silver leaf. The dragon holds in his claws this immense chandelier which, I suppose, is about 30 feet in depth."

My tour went on in this way for some hours, as Mr. Musgrave took pains to provide me with the details of the palace's artwork, porcelain, silver, furniture, and candelabra. After we concluded, I ducked into Chatfields, a noisy, beer-soaked pub filled with working people who liked to drink and be entertained by Bobby Banks, perhaps a prototypical English beer-hall entertainer. He led the crowd in a rousing chorus of "It's a Long Way to Tipperary" and "Come 'Round Any Old Time." As the sun set, I boarded the train back for London.

George IV was the king destined to reign over an empire that had recently lost thirteen colonies in America. He stayed on in Brighton, carrying on as scandalously as his

gout would allow. He is still best remembered for that fantastic palace and for the
fact that he promoted the novel idea that
people in society should take baths and
keep clean. He was also the first to demand
that his shoes be made to custom-fit the
right and left foot; previously, shoes had
been interchangeable. Well, Brighton in
1963 was no longer that fashionable, but its
postwar London visitors didn't seem to
care. Except for the rocks on the beach,
they liked it just fine.

Two Birminghams

One of the biggest stories I covered in my career—one of the biggest stories, in fact, in modern American history—was the civil rights movement of the early 1960s. I had grown up in the South, in a city shaped by segregation, and when I was a boy I hardly noticed it. No one in my family seemed to think there was anything wrong with the system. Nor did most white people in the South. But by the early sixties, black southerners had become fed up with segregation, sick of hearing white people say it was in their best interest, fed up with the daily indignities and the frequent violence that had maintained segregation for decades.

I started covering the civil rights movement in 1955, the year the Montgomery bus boycott began, and I continued covering it for over ten years. As a southerner, I felt I understood something of the way in which whites reacted to the movement; as someone who had by then lived in Washington for over a decade, I also understood how the rest of the country now looked at the South. I could see how the massive resisters and the Citizens' Councilors looked, to nonsouthern eyes, like bigoted yokels. And gradually, I also began to understand the way in which black southerners—whom I had always considered so kind, and friendly, and undemanding—had developed such terrible and justifiable resentments against the way we had treated them.

For me, the movement reached its zenith in Birmingham, Alabama, in 1963. Martin Luther King Jr. and the Southern Christian Leadership Council had brought their campaign against Jim Crow to a city that was thought to be one of the most defiant strongholds of the old system. Day after day, we reported on the stories of demonstrators and the hostility they encountered. Bull Connor, the city's police commissioner, a thick-necked bigot, was almost a caricature of a corrupt southern sheriff. He turned fire hoses and German shepherds on Birmingham's black citizens for participating in the demonstrations, and it seemed as though every night we were broadcasting terrible film showing children and teenagers being knocked off their feet by the high-pressure water, or running in terror from vicious dogs. I wondered as I watched this stuff how anyone in Birmingham could imagine that the rest of the country would take Bull Connor's side. But many white southerners were by then so fired up with hatred of liberals and the federal government that they didn't really care what the rest of us thought.

The state's governor, George Wallace, was making hay out of his own defense of segregation (an issue to which he'd paid little attention earlier in his career, but which he now saw as an opportunity to build a bigger political future). He won great popularity by seeming to defy the Kennedy administration in attempting to block the court-ordered enrollment of black students in the University of Alabama, even though he never had any intention of actually going to jail. He stood in the doorway through which the black students were supposed to enter the university, walked up to a podium and microphone and cameras that he had helped arrange, gave a little speech, and then—by prearrangement with Attorney General Robert Kennedy, whom he had met with earlier in the day—stepped aside and let the students in.

Martin Luther King Jr.—who had a lot more to fear from a southern jail than Wal-

lace did—did not try to avoid getting arrested. Bull Connor's men gleefully hauled
him off, and he spent some time in the city
lockup, where he wrote his famous "Letter
from a Birmingham Jail," explaining why
he and so many others were risking their
lives—and, in the case of the four little girls
who died in the 1963 church bombing in
Birmingham, losing their lives—fighting
what had at the beginning seemed an almost hopeless cause. A way of life that most
whites, including me, had taken for granted
most of their lives—and that many blacks
hated but never imagined would change—
was crumbling before our eyes.

Later in 1963, I decided to take a look at
the way in which people were struggling
with racial questions in another Birmingham—Birmingham, England. The British
do not have a three-century history of
racial diversity in the way Americans do.
But in recent decades, they have begun to
experience a lot of immigration from various parts of their former empire, including large numbers of black people from the
Caribbean. And so at the same time that
President Kennedy was asking Congress to
pass legislation dismantling segregation,
the Tory government in London was persuading Parliament to pass a bill restrict-
ing immigration from within the British

Commonwealth—Pakistan, India, Australia, Canada, and the West Indies. This was a watershed moment in the history of Britain; previously, any resident of the Commonwealth could move within it as easily as Americans can move from state to state. The liberal British press and the opposition Labour Party described this as a blatant attempt by the Conservatives to curb the growth of Britain's nonwhite population, but 90 percent of the people supported the bill. So I went to see what I could find out about the issue, and to compare the British problem with ours.

Birmingham is located near the geographic center of England, about 110 miles northwest of London. Birmingham today, I'm told, is a very different and much more attractive place than it was in the 1960s. But it was then the country's second largest city, an unlovely but important industrial center specializing in machine tools, engineering, and the metal trades. Birmingham was pounded by the Germans during World War II, but it made a surprisingly quick recovery. Its nickname was the "City of 1,001 Trades," and it was a magnet for workers from other parts of Great Britain and from the Commonwealth. By the early 1960s, many new workers were arriving in Birmingham from the West Indies.

The West Indies, a chain of islands in the Caribbean, is one of the more beautiful parts of the British Empire. The islands all look like tourist posters: white beaches, palms, blue water, perfect weather. But for many of the people who live there, they are places with terrible problems: lack of money, lack of jobs, and too many people with nothing to do. As the minister of development in Jamaica told me, "We have to export 16,000 people a year to beat the unemployment and population problem. We must have an escape hatch for an expanding population." Until 1962 the escape hatch was Britain. In 1959, 16,000 West Indians left for England, the following year 50,000, and in 1961, 70,000. Looking at these figures and at the arriving shiploads of West Indians, Indians, and Pakistanis, the British Home Office suddenly got scared that immigrants would overwhelm England. After an ugly public debate, the Commonwealth Immigration Bill was signed into law. It said that, as of June 30, 1962, no Commonwealth citizens could enter England unless they had jobs and housing in advance of arrival, could pass a stringent health test, and had no criminal record. As the deadline got closer, there was a frantic crush of people trying to get into Britain before the gates closed. One planeload from Pakistan made it with four minutes to spare; others missed the deadline by one or two minutes and were turned away.

At the time of my visit, Birmingham had 10,000 unemployed people living there, and the city leaders wanted no more new arrivals, which made for short tempers among the immigrant working classes. I spoke with a Jamaican carpenter named David Thompson, who typified the West Indian expat. He planned to earn a lot of money, he said, educate his children, and then go home. The soothing lilt of his island accent seemed altogether out of place in this gray, damp city. He admitted to a feeling of chronic homesickness. "When I came to England at first I saw a place looking somewhat very strange," he told me. "It was very cold, bitterly cold, and I tell you for a West Indian, I find it very, very hard. My ambition is not to stay here for more than five years. I think five years will be my limit because I want to go home to do a little farming, to look for good friends, and to have some nice times around the seacoast—sitting under coconut trees and looking at the beautiful sunset. I'm wishing for the day that I'll return back home." One reason blacks in Birmingham and elsewhere didn't fight harder against the new bill and the other problems they encountered is that, like David Thompson, they didn't really expect to stay. But of course, many of them ultimately did.

Some of the Birmingham officials I met with seemed to be trying very hard to help immigrants adjust to English society. Alan Gibbes ran a special welfare office just for the nonwhite immigrants. He admitted that it was not an easy job, since Birmingham attracted the lion's share of new arrivals. "The city council," he explained, "is quite determined that there shall be integration, and not segregation. Never do we want to see areas of the city bottled off and marked down as a West Indian center, or a Pakistani center, and the like. No, we're determined as far as we possibly can to get to the place where the colored people merge with the community as a whole and they become the new Birmingham citizens of tomorrow." Gibbes was a decent man, sensitive to the hardships that immigrants faced as they left familiar customs, and often their families, behind. He told me that he admired the courage of these "black Englishmen," as he called them, adding that they wanted nothing more than to be "a Brummie," the vernacular term for a resident of Birmingham.

In spite of its good efforts, Gibbes's office did not have much impact. The unions—

predominantly white—froze the immigrants out, and employers would hire them in only small numbers. So many Jamaicans had menial jobs, or none, and some worked as strikebreakers, which won them no friends among white workers. Landlords in all but the worst neighborhoods were reluctant to rent to West Indians, so they tended to congregate among themselves, forming in one neighborhood a sort of club they called the West Indian Federation Association. I went there one afternoon to talk to several men about their experiences as "black Brummies." There was a consensus that the British hadn't been receptive to their arrival, and that the West Indians were often taken for Africans, instead of loyal British subjects. Others complained that the Birmingham police refused to get involved in disputes among West Indians, leaving their neighborhoods vulnerable to crime. I heard, too, that white people had very little to do with the West Indians, in anything more than commercial transactions. Even though the West Indians had heard a lot about race friction before they left the Caribbean, they were still astonished to find that it actually existed when they arrived, and that the jobs and houses open to them were generally those the white people didn't want.

To learn something about the political thinking behind this situation, I went to London to talk to Sir Cyril Osborne, one of the more energetic and vocal Conservative advocates of the Commonwealth Immigration Bill, and Barbara Castle, an articulate Labourite and critic of Osborne. What I heard from them was remarkably similar to debates about the civil rights movement raging at home in America. I asked Osborne what he most wanted to achieve with the enactment of England's tougher immigration law. "I wanted to prevent England from being completely flooded by immigrants," he said, "whether they are black or white." He admitted that, arithmetically, nonwhite immigrants would bear the weight of the restrictions since they represented the lion's share of the Commonwealth's population. "I think this is the most difficult, the most dangerous, the most explosive problem our country has faced in three hundred years," he concluded solemnly. His position, he insisted, was grounded in a desire to protect England's economy and way of life for Anglo-Saxons, and he heatedly rejected any suggestion that his was a bigoted stance. "The basis of the whole problem is this. We are living at a standard of ten to fifteen times higher than the colored people in the Far East. This is a honey pot to which they come! I would come here if I were a colored man. You would too, if you had any sense."

When I visited Barbara Castle, I asked her if this bill was, in fact, an effort to keep out black people. "I haven't the slightest doubt that it is a color-bar bill," she answered. "I haven't the slightest doubt in my own mind that the government has just capitulated to racial prejudice which people like Cyril Osborne, I'm sorry to say, have helped encourage."

Castle told me that there had been brewing among a group in the House of Commons a demagogic chatter warning of an impending flood of migrants from the far reaches of the Commonwealth. "Well, the only snag to that argument is that we've had an open door for the last century, and we haven't been flooded yet." She complained that the doors to England had been locked without the gathering of any quantitative evidence to prove the Conservatives' dire forecasts. "The nearest estimate that we have is something like less than one percent of the population of this country is permanently colored. Now if we, the center of a multiracial Commonwealth, can't absorb this one percent without having a racial crisis, then there isn't much hope for the future peace of the world."

Osborne challenged her optimism. "The open door policy was all right," he said, "so long as it was not abused. In recent years, transportation and technology have enabled the door to be pushed wider and wider apart, and more and more people have come through it." Try as he might, Osborne could not hide his ideological conception of immigrants as savages at the gate. "The fact that the colored peoples of the world are becoming more conscious that they are the disinherited naturally makes them want to come here," he said, before turning the conversation back to America's imperfect past. "At one time you had the open door. Today you don't. Why? In order to protect the standard of living of your own people. Having seen the immense difficulties that your people faced, I did not want it here." The longer I let Osborne speak, the closer I got to his greatest fear. "I'm on record as having said that if the flood continued, this country would cease to be an Anglo-Saxon country, and it could well be that the Europeans would say we were no longer a European nation, and wouldn't want us."

Castle found Osborne's words appalling, particularly with the memory of Hitler's extermination camps so vivid and so close in time. "I think it's just terrifying to hear this sort of thing said today," she said. "This is why the bill is so inexcusable. Any pandering to that kind of attitude, with whatever excuses may be attached, is really opening the gates to fascism again."

In Hyde Park, at Speakers' Corner, crowds gathered for weeks on end listening to grassroots commentary while Parliament debated the bill. At times the crowds became overly exercised, particularly when one fellow, a West Indian who called himself Sir Robert Victor Matthews, took the soapbox. His tirades invited hecklers and then the policemen, amidst his own shouts of "This is my country!"

Birmingham, England, had one of the heaviest concentrations of black people in the nation. When I visited there in the early 1960s, they numbered about 8 percent of the population. Americans living in Birmingham, Alabama, where black Americans represented 30 percent of residents, or in Washington, D.C., where the figure was 60 percent, no doubt wondered what the British were worried about. But what struck me most was this: the sounds, words, and phraseology of race friction, whether spoken in an Alabama accent or a British accent, sound about the same.

EVENTS

Political Conventions

I covered a total of twenty-four national political conventions from 1952 to 1996, and a great many more presidential campaigns, and for much of that time I found them the most interesting and exciting part of my job—the conventions above all. Most of us in broadcasting have always loved live television, where anything can happen and where the spontaneity and unpredictability are like shots of adrenaline. And for many years nothing was more spontaneous and unpredictable than the rowdy, chaotic, ridiculous, and endlessly entertaining political conventions.

For more than 150 years, like an impatient Brigadoon, the convention came to life every four years. For much of that time, it was master of its own rules, and its decisions were irrevocable and often momentous. Yet, the convention isn't even mentioned in the Constitution or in any law ever passed by Congress. It sprang up, almost organically, out of the rich soil of American politics, and it grew and flourished for decades until that soil began to grow barren. Eventually, the convention grew barren as well.

Before there were nominating conventions, presidential candidates were selected by closed congressional caucuses. There were few roads, few newspapers, and little communication among states in the earliest days of the Republic, and political parties were not yet well developed. So Congress took over the job. The hero of the 1815 Battle of New Orleans, General Andrew Jackson, changed all that. The refusal of "King Caucus" to nominate Jackson in 1824, and the victory that year of the caucus candidate John Quincy Adams (even though Jackson received by far the highest popular vote), raised such a clatter that Congress gave up nominating power to a new institution, known as the convention. To Jackson and his supporters, and to many others, the convention seemed a more democratic way to nominate a candidate. It would be a great meeting of "the people," who could, the Jacksonians thought, be better trusted than elected officials to make good decisions.

The creation of the convention did not by itself create modern campaigns. Before the revolution in American communications in the twentieth century, it was entirely possible (and usually advisable) to hide the candidate himself during the campaign. In 1840, William Henry Harrison's campaign chief counseled his party managers: "Let him say not one single word about his principles or his creed—let him say nothing—promise nothing. Let no committee, no convention, no town meeting ever extract from him a single word about what he thinks now or will do hereafter. Let the use of pen and ink be wholly forbidden." The silent Harrison beat his more exposed opponent, President Martin Van Buren, handily. Contrast that to the first campaign I covered, over a century later in 1948, when Harry Truman said: "I expect to travel all over the country and talk at every whistle stop. We are going to be on the road most of the time from Labor Day to the end of the campaign." Truman's tireless touring—combined with Tom Dewey's stately, remote, almost nineteenth-century campaign—led Truman back to the White House.

In other ways, though, the campaigns of
the 1830s and 1840s were beginning to
become more like Truman's, and not just
because of the conventions. The fact that
no one heard from Harrison in 1840 didn't
mean that his campaign was silent. The
country was taken by storm with parades,
cider parties, songfests, and huge floats that
rolled from one city to another, as well as
badges, sashes, and lithographs galore. By
the time Harrison's victory came, his defeated rival, Van Buren, commented sor-
rowfully that he had been "lied down,
drunk down, and sung down." Eighty percent of eligible voters (who then included
only white men) voted that year.

Campaign verbiage today seems pallid by
contrast to the loud and boisterous political rhetoric of the nineteenth century. One
historian has written, "Advertising men
have had a hand in recent campaigns, but
politicians, untrained in their magic, knew
about projecting images when Madison
Avenue was a cow path." In 1840, politicians, not advertisers, crafted images as
effective as—and no more accurate than—
any that advertisers and consultants have
created in our time. William Henry Harrison became in 1840 the candidate of
the "Log Cabin and Hard Cider," a "people's candidate" in contrast to Martin Van

Buren, who was accused of eating in the White House off dishes made of gold. In reality, Harrison was the candidate of the Whig Party, which represented the interests of moneyed elites. And Harrison himself was a frontier aristocrat who drank good bourbon, lived on a two-thousand-acre estate, and as far as anyone knows never saw the inside of a log cabin.

The invention of the telegraph slowly changed the process of reporting events. In 1844, Washington politicos were amazed to get the news from the Democratic convention in Baltimore, just as it was happening: the convention nominated James K. Polk (the first "dark horse") for president. Gradually, conventions became events that Americans no longer read about a week or two later in their newspapers, but could follow day by day, even hour by hour, through telegraphic reporting. It was at that same convention, by the way, that a platform condemned "fictitious symbols" and "displays and appeals insulting to the judgment and subversive of the intellect of the people," one of the first of many failed efforts to exhort politicians to put more "substance" in their campaigns.

Among the candidacies to emerge from conventions, there have been some genuine surprises. Possibly no man was more thoroughly shocked at the suggestion of his running than Zachary Taylor. When a visitor to Taylor's tent on a Mexican War battlefield in 1848 toasted him as the next president of the United States, Taylor told him, "Stop your nonsense and drink your whiskey." But a few months later, the Whig Party—once again desperate for a candidate with the broad popular appeal that their most important leaders did not have—plucked the war hero Taylor up and made him their candidate. Almost without thinking, they tacked Millard Fillmore, a little-known ex-congressman from New York, onto the ticket as the vice presidential nominee. Taylor was a southerner, and Fillmore was a sop to the North. The Whig leaders who chose him lived to regret their decision when Taylor died after a year and a half in office, and Fillmore became president and wrecked the party. "God save us from Whig vice presidents!" an Ohio Whig later said. But a century and more later, most conventions—and most presidential candidates—continued to treat the vice presidency as a kind of casual afterthought.

However surprised Taylor might have been when he was nominated in 1848, the whole country reacted with disbelief in 1852, when the Democratic Party nominated Franklin Pierce, an obscure New Hampshire senator. Stephen Douglas said at the time, "Hereafter, no private citizen is safe." Pierce became the nominee because party leaders were divided about the more prominent candidates. They compromised on the bland and unthreatening Pierce, who went on to become one of the worst presidents in American history, despite a laudatory campaign biography by Nathaniel Hawthorne. Conventions clearly were not much more reliable than the caucuses in choosing presidential candidates of stature. But they were a lot more fun, and they were popular with the electorate, many of whom followed them the way Americans today follow professional sports.

The earliest nominating conventions were closed to outsiders, but, eventually, the public was not only admitted but was commandeered for support. In 1860, Abraham Lincoln's champion, Norman Judd, without Lincoln's knowledge, insured a sizable cheering section by counterfeiting tickets to the gallery and giving them to Lincoln supporters—practices that became standard parts of convention tactics through the 1960s.

Nineteenth-century campaigns generated more popular interest, and produced

much higher voter turnout, than campaigns do today. They were also more vit-
riolic, by far, which raises some questions
about the conventional wisdom of our time
that voters stay away from the polls because
of negative campaigning. In 1884, the main
issue of the presidential election seemed to
be Grover Cleveland's illegitimate child
versus James G. Blaine's corruption—and
his apparent tolerance of a slur on Catholics
from one of his supporters, a Protestant
clergyman who referred to the Democrats
as the party of "rum, Romanism, and re-
bellion." This was the election of "Blaine!
Blaine! James G. Blaine! The continental
liar from the State of Maine!" and "Ma!
Ma! Where's my pa! He's gone to the
White House, ha, ha, ha!" Seventy-eight
percent of the electorate voted that year.

That election, by the way, was very
close. And when the tightness of the New
York vote held up the returns for several
days, New York City's Western Union office was stormed by mobs calling for the
company president's neck, shouting "Hang
Jay Gould!" The legacy of that threat was
one big reason that, decades later, radio
and television reporters, including me,
wasted no time in relaying the returns to
viewers—and one reason for the networks'

disastrous mistake in calling Florida prematurely after the 2000 election.

With rare exceptions, nineteenth-century candidates didn't actively campaign (the theory being that "the office seeks the man"). They never appeared at conventions. (The first presidential nominee to do that was Franklin Roosevelt in 1932.) Instead, they waited at home for a "notification committee" to call on them and "inform" them of the results, information they received with disingenuous surprise and humility. After that, a candidate rarely left his house, except to appear occasionally on the front porch to make a bland, careful speech to one or another visiting delegation. One exception was the populist candidate in 1892, General James Weaver, who stumped the West to urge farmers to throw out the people who were keeping farm prices low and the price of money high. Another exception (and another loser) was William Jennings Bryan, who, four years later, was the nominee of both the Democratic and the Populist conventions. He made more than six hundred speeches in twenty-nine states, while William McKinley blithely received visits from delegates at his Ohio home. McKinley won handily.

. . .

But the days of boss control of conventions and front-porch campaigns were numbered. Party primaries, which allowed voters and not bosses to select delegates to the conventions, were beginning to spread across the country. Most delegates were still chosen by the party machinery. Not until the 1970s did the primaries fully determine the parties' presidential nominees. But beginning in the first decade of the twentieth century, party nominees had to show at least some strength in popular primaries to be credible candidates in the fall. In 1912, President William Howard Taft lost every Republican primary to former president Theodore Roosevelt. Party leaders still controlled enough delegations to win him the nomination, but he had been so discredited in the eyes of the voters that year that he received only 23 percent of the vote and came in third (behind Woodrow Wilson and TR, who ran as the candidate of the new Progressive Party).

Campaigning had changed too. By the early twentieth century, the railroad train had come into its own as a traveling podium. Because the Populists couldn't afford the luxury of special trains, they had tried to stop other parties from using them

in the 1890s. Populist-controlled legisla-
tures of several western states passed laws
prohibiting political gatherings closer than
200 feet to a track, thus eliminating ad-
dresses from the rear platforms of trains.
Some of those laws were still in force in
the first decades of the twentieth century,
long after the Populist Party was gone. But
party leaders were not to be thwarted.
They set up platforms 200 feet or more
from the tracks and had local orators address the crowds until the candidate's train
pulled in. A carriage would then whisk the
main speaker from train to platform. At the
sound of the train whistle, he'd be trans-
ported back just as rapidly. Thus was born
the "whistle-stop" campaign.

The physical appearance of politicos was
a strong factor long before they came under the scrutiny of television. Over eighty
years ago, Charles Evans Hughes trimmed
the "forest of his beard" in answer to critics who charged that it hid the personality
of the candidate. It was a postelection suggestion from an eleven-year-old girl that
persuaded another Republican, Abraham
Lincoln, to let his whiskers grow. And perhaps the most famously inept of all American presidents, Warren G. Harding, was
chosen for the Republican Party's nomination in 1920 not just because he was "a

good second-rater," as one of his supporters put it, but also because, as another one
said, "he looks like a president." In this
case, looks were definitely deceiving.

The first convention to be broadcast (and
nearly the last) was the Democratic get-
together of 1924 in New York City, the
longest on record. That was the affair in
which the head of the Alabama delegation
began every roll call with the same words:
"Alabama casts twenty-four votes for Un-
derwood." Not until the 103rd ballot was
a deadlock between Al Smith and William
G. McAdoo broken. John W. Davis, a
bland corporate lawyer, was nominated to
run, and lose, against Coolidge.

That same convention marked the first
major battle between broadcasting and the
press. After eighty-six ballots, H. L.
Mencken wired the *Baltimore Sun,* "Everything is uncertain in this convention but
one thing: John W. Davis will never be
nominated." Next day, when radio reported the Democrats' agreement on
Davis, Mencken was aghast. "Why, that's
incredible!" he said. "I have already sent
off a story that it's impossible. I wonder if
those idiots back in Baltimore will know
enough to strike out the 'never.'" They
didn't. The conventions of the twenties
evoked this classic evaluation of the two

major political parties by the *New York Times*'s Arthur Krock: "Democrats are excitable, difficult to lead, idealistic, and reckless when in Convention assembled. History demonstrates that they would rather fight among themselves than with the enemy. When Republican delegations are released from their home instructions, they go to their bosses. When Democratic delegations are released, they go to pieces."

In 1928 nationwide radio facilities were first used extensively in a campaign. "Brown Derby" Al Smith emerged the loser against "High Collar" Herbert Hoover. While many explanations have been offered for the result, not a few experts have attributed Smith's defeat in part to his pronounced New Yorkese delivery. In the past, only the small number of Americans who had watched a candidate deliver a speech had ever heard his voice. Now, radio carried voices across the nation. Would Theodore Roosevelt, who had a high squeaky voice that contradicted his tough masculine image, have done as well in the age of radio?

If radio did, indeed, work to Hoover's advantage in that campaign, it boomeranged against him four years later. In 1932, Franklin Roosevelt—once it was clear that he would be the Democratic

Party's nominee—got on an airplane (the first presidential candidate ever to do so), flew to Chicago, and accepted the nomination in a speech before the convention. It was important for Roosevelt to appear vigorous and dynamic because he was confined to a wheelchair, something many Americans did not know. And so in Chicago, as elsewhere, he arranged to have himself wheeled to a curtain a few yards away from the podium, and then—his legs held up with rigid steel braces, one arm clenching a cane and the other the arm of his son—he "walked" to the podium and gave an unforgettable speech in which he pledged "a new deal for the American people." That and the Depression might well have been too much for *any* opponent.

The first televised convention was in 1948, a year in which the relatively few people who owned television sets also watched coverage of the primaries, the campaigns, and the election itself on their home screens. Once staged exclusively for the delegates, from this point on the conventions would increasingly be produced with an eye for the millions across the nation. After the war, public interest in the conventions was high and remained high for twenty years. Of course, this coincided with the emergence of the United States as the leading superpower, the wealthiest and most democratic nation in the world. People felt good about the country and thought its political institutions were important.

In 1948 both parties gathered in Philadelphia. The Republicans were first, and thus the first to see strange new cameras staring at them. Viewers outside the hall were able to view the tedious process of Thomas E. Dewey, the crime-busting governor of New York, whom Alice Roosevelt Longworth, TR's daughter, described as looking like "the little man on a wedding cake," finally winning the nomination, after three ballots, over the old-guard Senator Robert A. Taft of Ohio; Harold Stassen, the former governor of Minnesota and career candidate for president; and Earl Warren, then the governor of California.

The Republicans had no clue about how to behave in front of the television cameras, and we had no clue about how to cover a convention. None of our crew at NBC had ever broadcast one. The most important story of the 1948 convention was the contest for the nomination, of course, which went to Tom Dewey, the prohibitive favorite who in the end shockingly lost the election to Truman. But because of the cameras, we kept too glued to what was happening in the hall itself, which for the most part was a lot of socializing and demonstrating, while the real decisions were being made elsewhere.

When the Democrats came to town the show was better, but our coverage of it wasn't. This was the first convention in sixteen years in which Roosevelt was not the nominee. Harry Truman, who had succeeded FDR, was seeking the nomination. But the party was not behind him in the way it had been behind Roosevelt. A number of delegates wore buttons saying "We're Just Mild About Harry." The convention was a tumultuous one. The left didn't like him because he wasn't as dynamic as Roosevelt and because some of them (including some Communists) didn't like his tough Cold War policies against the Soviet Union. Some of them left the party and supported Henry Wallace's Progressive Party candidacy that fall. The southern right wing didn't like Truman because of his mild support for civil rights. They walked out of the convention and formed the States' Rights ("Dixiecrat") Party with Governor Strom Thurmond

of South Carolina as its presidential nominee. Thurmond called Truman a "carpetbagger" who would destroy the American
way of life by ending segregation. So there
was plenty to report on, but our primitive
coverage made watching it more tiresome
than reading about it in the newspapers.
John Cameron Swayze and the cameraman
were still up in the rafters, and because he
was trained to read carefully scripted news
reports, Swayze was unable to ad-lib in response to unplanned events. It was not an
auspicious start to the era of televised political conventions.

By 1952 we had gotten our act together
a little more. Television had grown enormously since the previous conventions,
with TV sets now in seventeen million
homes, so there was much more incentive
to get it right. The parties allowed us to
have cameras on the floor, but they soon
regretted it. During the frequent dull moments, Bob Doyle, the director of the
NBC coverage, had his cameramen roam
around the hall looking for shots that
would hold the interest of the audience.
We broadcast close-ups of delegates sleep-
ing, eating like pigs, acting like fools, and
paying no attention to the speakers. (We
also broadcast a picture from Washington
of my son Joel, born during the conven-

tion. My first view of him was on the TV monitor at the convention.)

Soon it became apparent that the Republicans cared more about how they looked on television than the Democrats. Republican delegates began to improve their behavior. They sat in their seats and listened respectfully to the speakers. They cleaned up after themselves and maintained a well-mannered appearance. Democrats, on the other hand, continued to behave like schoolchildren during recess. They ran around the aisles schmoozing, enjoying themselves, and making a mess, heedless that millions of Americans were watching them. During one speech I used binoculars to see how many delegates were paying attention—I couldn't find any.

When it came time to plan for the 1956 conventions, NBC decided it needed anchors who knew how to narrate over a television picture. Chet Huntley was a natural: he was experienced and telegenic. But there was some debate about who Huntley's partner would be. Julian Goodman, a good friend of mine and the manager of the Washington bureau, nominated me, and after a long debate within the upper levels of NBC, Goodman got his way.

Some people at NBC wanted to turn the political conventions into pure entertainment. Huntley and I resisted this impulse, but we were always aware of the tension between treating the conventions as serious news and making them interesting to watch, and we realized that audiences would not sit still for the serious stuff unless we gave them something entertaining as well. I became known for my ad-libbing during dull moments, when I would relay some little fact or anecdote. Those supposed ad-libs were designed to cut the boredom and hold the viewers' attention, but they were a result of extensive research we had done on every person, every candidate, every state chairman, every issue that might come before the convention delegates. I might have been naive, but I thought that serious news could be presented in an entertaining way, and that's what I tried to do at the conventions.

In 1956, our operations were still fairly crude. We sat in a plywood and beaverboard studio somewhere away from the convention floor. The idea was for us to look only at the TV picture to make sure that what we were saying matched what the viewers were seeing. But it was a stupid idea. Huntley and I sat in this little studio and worked entirely from a TV monitor. We couldn't see the hall at all, and so we had no sense of the feeling of the convention, what was really going on down on the floor. Beginning in 1960, the networks built big glass boxes high above the convention floor so that we could see everything below—and so that everyone below could see us. I don't know if anyone thought of it this way, but the anchor booths were like an announcement from the networks that they were the power at conventions now.

As unsophisticated as we were with the new medium, the politicians were even worse. Paul Dever, former governor of Massachusetts, made a speech, and he did not understand what now is generally understood. He was talking to a tremendous hall full of people, therefore he felt the need to shout, as if he were speaking to a huge outdoor crowd without a microphone or cameras. But in a close-up on the television screen, he looked completely mad. He was sweating and screaming and he looked like a fool.

The politicians got wiser, not only about presenting themselves on television but also about controlling television. At first they tried to keep the cameras out entirely. When that became impossible they tried to tell us what to show and how to show it. In the 1960s, the Republican Party attempted to keep us from showing the nastiness of the fights between the old-line, country-club party members and the new right wing. During the 1964 Republican convention in San Francisco, former president Eisenhower denounced us for televising right-wing delegates booing and heckling Nelson Rockefeller and his wife. But by then we were sufficiently established to be able to show whatever was happening on the floor; and in 1964, some of what was happening was pretty ugly.

The right wing had developed a theory that all of us in the media were agents of the Soviet Union. They hated us with an uncontrolled fury that was frightening to watch, especially when we were in the same room with them. When Eisenhower defended Barry Goldwater against the "sensation-seeking columnists and commentators," the convention hall erupted into a hateful mob scene. Delegates leapt out of their chairs and rushed toward the network booths, which were, thankfully, way up in the rafters. They stood underneath us, shouting and shaking their fists. I don't think they would have actually lynched us, but I was glad to be out of their reach. When I went back to the hotel after the sessions—the same hotel where the Goldwater headquarters was located—I had to pass through a lobby thronged with people wearing lapel buttons saying "Stamp Out Huntley Brinkley." Some of them heckled me as I walked by, but no one did more than that. Still, it was an unnerving experience.

In 1964 the Democrats were just as concerned about presenting a united front as were their opponents. At their convention in Atlantic City, race was a major and divisive issue, as it had been in the party since before the Civil War. A racially mixed group called the Mississippi Freedom Democratic Party, led by Fannie Lou Hamer, came to Atlantic City to challenge the all-white delegation from Mississippi, which had been selected in a nominating process that excluded blacks. Eventually, with the help of Martin Luther King Jr., a compromise was worked out whereby the civil rights group would be seated as observers, with promises of party reforms later on, while the regular party delegates would keep their seats. The convention itself voted to accept this, but the rival Mississippi delegations both walked out of the convention in disgust.

The fight over race may have hurt the Democrats, but it helped the television ratings, especially ours. When the figures came in, they showed such a huge share for NBC that the network rechecked them several times to make sure they were accurate. They showed that at one point during the convention, we had 84 percent of the audience, probably a record in broadcasting history.

More than the Democrats, the Republicans learned from their 1964 experience about the importance of the television coverage of their conventions. In 1968 Eisenhower recommended that the party ban the press from the convention floor, to keep it from showing embarrassing images of the delegates. But more clever Republicans decided to use television rather than fight it. They realized that broadcast coverage of their convention was an opportunity for massive free advertising. The Republicans staged their 1968 convention entirely for TV, which made it almost completely boring. The only interesting moment came when there was a fight over whether to eject Representative H. R. Gross from the hall. Gross was a leading member of the Neanderthal wing of the party and was completely deaf to public opinion. When Jackie Kennedy had asked that a perpetual flame be placed at the grave of her husband in 1963, Gross had opposed it. In a speech on the floor of the House, he had demanded to know how much the Eternal Flame would cost. People were seen wearing buttons reading "H. R. Gross Certainly Is." In an effort to clean up the party's image, several Republicans introduced a resolution to force Gross out of the convention and replace him with a housewife from Des Moines. The resolution failed on a tie vote, but not long after, Iowans voted Gross out of office.

Divisions at the Democratic convention in 1968 were deeper, more violent, and much more dramatic. Opposition to the Vietnam War had become a mass movement, and the prowar leaders of the Democratic Party were the objects of much of the rage. Before the convention even started, the movement had forced Lyndon Johnson to withdraw from the presidential race. In fact, he could barely show his face in public and didn't even make an appearance at the convention that year— although he never stopped trying to fix things and never stopped hoping that somehow the party would come to its senses and nominate him again. He had dozens of people in Chicago planning a big birthday celebration for him at the convention hall, but at the last minute he decided not to go—maybe because so many people were telling him that he would not find a friendly crowd in the gallery or, for that matter, on the floor.

Johnson had thrown his support, though less than wholeheartedly, to Hubert Humphrey, who vowed to continue the war despite the polls showing that 60 to 70 percent of the public had turned against it as unwinnable and too costly in lives. For a time, it looked as though Robert Kennedy—who had turned against the war that he and his brother, the president, had once managed—might take the nomination away from Humphrey. But after Kennedy's death, Humphrey's only opponents were George McGovern and Eugene McCarthy, both of whom promised to pull the United States out of Vietnam if elected, but neither of whom had any broad support within the party, which was still substantially controlled by local machines and bosses.

When the convention started, it appeared that the war had come to Chicago. The convention hall, the International Amphitheater at the Stockyards, several miles from downtown, was surrounded on all sides by chain-link fencing and barbed wire, 11,900 Chicago policemen, 7,500 U.S. Army troops, 7,500 Illinois National Guardsmen, and 1,000 agents from the FBI and the Secret Service. They were there to protect the convention from the thousands of antiwar protesters, mostly young people, who were streaming into the city. The mayor, Richard J. Daley, declared that he would crush any attempts to disrupt the convention.

At the convention hall itself, the security was almost as bad as the demonstrators. Delegates and visitors had electronic badges that were supposed to be read by machines at the doors, but the machines didn't work. Security officials sometimes tried to bar people with legitimate credentials, and some fights broke out. Several miles away, in Lincoln and Grant Parks downtown, where most of the demonstrators were, the police attacked the protesters with clubs and tear gas. The clouds of gas grew so large that they even seeped into the stately lobby of the Conrad Hilton, where delegates were staying. The police were trying to stop an unsanctioned effort by the protesters to march through the streets to the International Amphitheater. Hundreds of young people were bloodied and had their heads split open when the police plowed into them with clubs swinging. The police later announced that 589 people had been arrested and 100 demonstrators and 119 policemen had been injured. No one believed the figures. It was the worst sight I had ever seen in my years of covering conventions, and

to this day the thing that most people remember most clearly about Chicago in
1968 was thousands of young people—
many of them with blood streaming down
their foreheads from the blows of police
billy clubs—chanting "The whole world is
watching." They knew we were there.

The scene inside the convention hall was
less violent but nearly as sordid. In a pathetic attempt to bolster his image, Daley
ordered city workers to pack the galleries
and carry cheap posters printed with the
words WE LOVE MAYOR DALEY. That didn't
help him much with the press. Virtually all
of us believed he had acted like a thug, and
we assumed most Americans would agree
with us. Only later did we discover that
the majority of television viewers sympa-
thized with Daley and the police, not with
the demonstrators, and that many of them
were furious with us for seeming to side
with the protesters.

Interest in the conventions declined
steadily after the 1960s, and many have
wondered why. I think in part it has to do
with the public's disillusionment with politics in general, but also with the way the
conventions have become parodies of
themselves. Leaders of the parties began to

look at the conventions as nothing more than opportunities to put forth their propaganda and make money. The 1984 Democratic convention in San Francisco was a good example. The proceedings in the hall were so tightly scripted that nothing unexpected happened. And the delegates themselves were reduced to simply an audience, like the guests at the taping of a television program. The convention hall was kept in near darkness so that the audience could see the giant television screens on either side of the podium, which meant that the delegates could not see one another, and our reporters could barely see them.

This was also the year that the central role of money in politics became most clearly visible. For five thousand dollars, visitors were given membership in a meaningless group called the Democratic National Convention Club, two seats in the convention hall, help with hotel reservations, and, most importantly, access to the VIP lounge and its free whiskey. Ten thousand dollars bought them an invitation to a dinner with several hundred people, including the presidential and vice presidential candidates. For a mere twenty-five thousand dollars, members got dinner and a reception with the candidates in a smaller group. And if they wanted to have their pictures taken with both nominees, the charge was one hundred thousand dollars. They might as well have hung up signs reading CLEARANCE SALE, EVERYTHING MUST GO.

A few years later, there was no longer even much of a pretense about the nature of conventions, and especially the Republican ones. Everything was for sale. At the 1992 GOP convention in Houston, I saw a woman wearing a huge mound of blond hair, driving a pink Cadillac convertible with the top down and carrying a Bible bound in mink fur. Never before had so many rich people been so ostentatiously on display at a political convention than at the Republican meetings of the 1980s and 1990s.

The last conventions I covered, in 1992 and 1996, were so uninteresting that the networks mostly gave up on them. At ABC, Peter Jennings and I came on for an hour or so late in the evening to sum up what had happened (usually nothing) and to show one or two featured speeches. Because there was so little time on the air, our floor reporters were almost invisible. By now the networks had stopped building the big glass booths perched up in the rafters. I finished my career covering conventions the same way I started, in a little plywood studio far from the convention hall, with no view of the proceedings except for a monitor.

Should we care that conventions are now completely stage-managed events with no more spontaneity than a movie? For those of us who covered the old messy meetings, the change was hard to take. But do voters really care? Most of them probably haven't noticed the change, and younger voters have never seen anything much different. I think, though, that the infomercial conventions of today are at least a small part of the reason that so many Americans have lost interest in politics and think that everything about our political system is phony and corrupt. The old conventions may have been chaotic and often ridiculous. They may have done damage from time to time to the parties and their candidates. But they showed politics as a living, breathing, brawling process—not the sterile, money-driven activity it so often is today.

A State Visit

One of the most common settings for the conduct of American foreign policy is the visit of a chief of state to Washington, D.C. These occur so frequently that hardly anyone notices them anymore. Today, there is very little about these visits that is visible to the public. Chiefs of state generally arrive on military planes at Andrews Air Force Base, out of sight of the public and, usually, the media. They stay in Blair House, the government's private guest house across from the White House, or in their own embassy's residence. Their public appearances consist of carefully staged photo opportunities in the Rose Garden or the Oval Office, a White House news conference, and sometimes a drive up to the Capitol to meet with members of Congress.

But not many decades ago, these visits were vivid spectacles requiring months of preparation and precise coordination among teams of people numbering in the hundreds. In 1963, shortly before the death of President Kennedy, I decided that it would be interesting to explore the preparations for a particularly interesting state visitor—the emperor who came to dinner, a man whose imperial title was the Elect of God, King of Kings, King of Zion, Conquering Lion of Judah, His Majesty Haile Selassie the First, Emperor of Ethiopia.

Haile Selassie was the son of a provincial governor in Ethiopia. Born in 1892, he was educated in a French Catholic mission and acquired dreams of imperial glory. As a young man, he was a successful businessman who used his wealth to acquire strategic contacts throughout Ethiopia and abroad. He also acquired imperial connections by marrying the emperor's great-granddaughter. When the sitting emperor, Menelik II, who had created much of what was now the Ethiopian "empire," died, Haile Selassie used his connections to arrange the overthrow of Menilek's chosen heir and instead installed Menelik's daughter, Zauditu, as a figurehead queen, with himself as "regent." He was twenty-six. In 1930, Zauditu died and Haile Selassie, who had already been the nation's real

ruler for fourteen years, proclaimed himself emperor.

By then, he was already a figure of considerable interest among Africans around
the world—a symbol to many of them of
the possibilities of African greatness. The
conspicuous symbols of imperial authority
that seemed so pompous to many white
westerners appeared to many Africans as
authentic evidence of his greatness. Haile
Selassie was a figure of cultish fascination
in the Caribbean, where he helped inspire
the Rastafarian movement, and even in
Harlem, where he was a hero to the Gar-
vey movement in the 1920s. After Mussolini invaded his country in 1935 and
dislodged him from his throne, his fame
grew even greater and he made a memorable plea to the League of Nations for assistance—although the League did nothing
in response.

After the war, back on the throne, he
profited, ironically, from the many invest-
ments in infrastructure and industry the
Italians had made during their brief occupation of the country. And in 1955 he
created what he considered a modern constitution, which established a parliament
and a cabinet, but which also affirmed his
own absolute power. By 1963, he was
starting to be in some trouble at home.

There had been an unsuccessful coup attempt in 1960, and there was strong international opposition to his annexation of
Eritrea in 1962, in violation of a United
Nations mandate. So his state visit to the
United States (which had supported the
annexation) was an important event for
him in shoring up his shaky regime, which
was now forty-seven years old.

The story of the visit begins in the State
Department. If laid out in a straight line,
the corridors of the State Department
building in Foggy Bottom would run for
more than five miles, and it is there, for
many nations around the globe, that the
center of American power is located. This
was even more true in the 1960s, before
the emergence of the White House National Security Council as the center of
foreign policy power. From State's offices,
full of coffeemakers and copying machines,
the United States maintains diplomatic relations with dozens of countries. This is
where the aid money comes from; it is
from here that they will send out someone
to show you how to plant wheat or run a
bus line or build a dam; and here is the
place where they can decide to prop up a
weak government or let it collapse. And so,
it is where the leaders of small countries,
for reasons of prestige at home, ask to be

invited because they need their own people to see that they have come to Washington and been received and treated as
though they are important to the world's
most important power—whether they are
or not. And while this need is usually a little one-sided, it is not entirely so because
the United States isn't so powerful that it
doesn't need friends. This relationship between countries, and their mutual need for
each other, is particularly visible at the time
of the visit of a chief of state.

It falls to the State Department's Office
of Protocol to organize the feting of
these official visitors, whether it is a boiled
shirt, white-tie dinner at the White House
or a barbecue at the presidential ranch.
When Emperor Haile Selassie sent word
to Berhanou Dinke, his ambassador in
Washington, that he would like President
Kennedy to invite him to the White
House, the first person to hear about it was
the chief officer of protocol, Ambassador
Angier Biddle Duke. In the initial meeting between Ambassador Dinke and Ambassador Duke, the basics were laid out
in simple language: President Kennedy
looked forward to this visit marking a
milestone in the relationship between the
two countries, Duke reported, but the
rules of protocol had changed a bit since

the emperor's previous trip to Washington in 1954. First, no more than ten persons could be included in the emperor's official party, meaning the group whose expenses would be paid for by the American government; and all unofficial persons—photographers and journalists, for example—should come at the emperor's (or their own) expense. Biographical information and six photographs should be provided to the State Department for each member of the official party, as well as information noting their proficiency in English, or other languages, their personal interests and dislikes, and dietary limitations. When the two ambassadors concluded their meeting, Duke gave the go-ahead to a protocol officer, who in turn caused the bureaucracy to begin to move, which means that he picked up the telephone and set more meetings into motion. Before it was all over, more than five hundred memoranda had been generated, and Ethiopia's Ambassador Dinke had trekked seven times to the State Department to confer with Ambassador Duke.

Official visitors to Washington usually fly from Andrews Air Force Base to the White House lawn by helicopter, but Haile Selassie, whose name meant "Might of the Trinity," thought this entry undignified for a man of his stature, and demanded that he arrive by train. After some head-scratching, the State Department decided that the emperor's jet should fly from Addis Ababa to Philadelphia, which is on the railroad's main line to Washington and had a schedule that could get the royal party to the capital on time, that being noon on October 1. A special meeting was arranged to discuss the logistics of the train's arrival, which had to be synchronized with the arrival of President Kennedy's limousine at Washington's Union Station. Actually, the directive called for the train to back into the station and dock at 11:59 a.m., and if that wasn't enough pressure to place on one engineer, he was required to line up the door from which the royal party would debark so that the emperor would step squarely onto a chalk mark on the red carpet to greet official Washington.

How and when to dock the train was just one small part of the planning. There were also preparations for a well-oiled delivery of pomp and circumstance: gun salutes, honor guards, military bands, a parade down Pennsylvania Avenue, the hanging of banners and flags, security details, and elaborate catered receptions, not to mention the White House state dinner. Haile Selassie did make another special request:

rather than visit the Tomb of the Unknown Soldier at Arlington Cemetery,
which was protocol for the time, His
Majesty wanted to lay a special silver
wreath at the Lincoln Memorial. Haile Selassie had, like Lincoln, emancipated the
slaves of his country, and so he felt an affinity for the sixteenth president. As for so
many other aspects of these preparations,
the wreath-laying required that the army
issue special order "NCASSE Change 1,
Visit to Washington, SOP, Arrival and De-
parture Ceremonies, Appendix I to Annex
F, Details of Wreath Ceremony." But the
various committees of the armed forces
took this and their other responsibilities in
stride because they had had lots of practice.
Just in the previous four years, eighty other
heads of state had similarly demanded their
attention.

So it was for Edgar Morris, chairman of
the Citizens' Reception Committee at the
District of Columbia's City Hall, a veteran
of sixty-nine state visits. When he got
word of Haile Selassie's visit, he promptly
called his people together and, in one
efficient sweep, placed his orders for an ad-
ditional seven hundred police, the decora-
tion of government buildings with the
Ethiopian flag, posters bearing the emperor's lion crest, and an immense seventy-

foot welcome banner to be hung from two fire ladders across Pennsylvania Avenue.

As October 1 drew close, State Department employees pulled the 140-foot red carpet out of storage for inspection, and began its arduous cleaning. The tradition of welcoming heads of state with carpets runs back over a thousand years—to Charlemagne, who declined to have his feet touch the ground. And with the imminent arrival of another emperor, the red carpet had to be in pristine condition. In a downtown theater, a sign painter got to work on the banner, chafing at the length of the greeting, which was to read: WELCOME HIS IMPERIAL MAJESTY HAILE SE-LASSIE I EMPEROR OF ETHIOPIA. Meanwhile, people in the protocol office busied themselves memorizing the names, photographs, and titles of all those traveling in the emperor's party, so that when they arrived, there would be no stumbling or groping in the introductions and conversation. And in various offices at the State Department, at the White House, and, in this particular instance, in the office of Chief Justice Earl Warren—who would host a luncheon for Selassie aboard the *Sequoia,* the secretary of the navy's yacht—a carefully coordinated and multilayered effort was undertaken to avoid menu duplication, mismatched wines, or other culinary faux pas, for several requisite and lavish banquets. The White House planned to serve beef for the state dinner, the State Department chose pheasant for its luncheon, and so forth. Guest lists had to be drawn up and scrutinized to avoid slighting anyone who was anyone, or thought they were. Elsewhere folks set to work lettering place cards and drawing up seating charts.

Finally, October 1 arrived, a brilliant autumn day. At 9:30 a.m., His Imperial Majesty, with Ambassador Duke in tow, climbed on a private railroad car in Philadelphia and began rolling southward toward Washington at seventy-five miles per hour. Riding in the emperor's private car were the members of his official party, limited to ten just as Ambassador Duke had requested: his cousin, his granddaughter, two government ministers, the keeper of his seal, his chief of staff, his aide-de-camp, his interpreter, his private secretary, and Ambassador Dinke. The emperor's son, who in 1960 joined a revolt against his father and tried to overthrow him, stayed home. As the train gathered steam, men hung flags in Washington, and carefully so, because the Ethiopian flag upside down is the Bolivian flag. (In fact, when Bolivia's president came to visit later, the same flags were used in reverse.) Police details walked the length of Pennsylvania Avenue, looking for bombs or loose manhole covers—although with somewhat less urgency than they might do so today. The fire department sent two trucks, which raised their ladders into an arch above the street so that twelve men, including firemen and stagehands, could manage the hanging of the welcome banner that had been painted in the theater. When I say that tempers flared, I am being charitable.

Across town at Union Station, the military began moving in at 8:30, bringing the red carpet and sprucing up the tracks. The entire navy band assembled at railside, as did an honor guard and a color guard comprising soldiers from all branches of the military. An enlisted fellow asked his coworker, "Who ever thought it'd be so tough to get a rug straight?" After the carpet was finally laid out, the nameplates of forty-three people who would stand in the receiving line were taped down along its border, beginning with the president and the First Lady, down to Edgar Morris of the Citizens' Reception Committee. The soldiers took on the responsibility for getting this right, using a list sent over by the protocol office.

Back on the train, Ambassador Duke,

speaking in French, attempted to point out for the emperor the scenic landmarks along the way to Washington, though on this route there are not very many. The emperor sat ramrod straight in his seat, a bit on edge. He was a thin, light-skinned man with high cheekbones, large round eyes, gray hair, and a closely cropped beard; he wore a dress field uniform of fine cotton khaki covered in ribbons and medals. A steady murmur of small talk filled the car, but no one really seemed engaged in conversation. Fifteen minutes before the train's scheduled arrival, an entire world of last-minute arrangements fell into place. A White House limousine pulled into Union Station, ready to take President Kennedy and the emperor down the parade route to the White House; the president, however, arrived at the last possible minute in yet another car. Out on Pennsylvania Avenue, the police cleared the parade route of traffic and conducted last-minute security sweeps. In the station, soldiers stood at the ready with walkie-talkies to signal the firing of the gun battery's twenty-one guns, at precisely three-second intervals. (Extra guns were on hand, in case one or more should misfire.) The red carpet got one last sweep just as the emperor's car began backing into the station. All of this was synchronized with the train's docking, and it was all timed just right—in fact, it was done perfectly.

As the emperor's car came to a standstill, the party onboard exhibited the strains of anticipation. Standing inside the car and looking out, the emperor and Ambassador Duke could see President Kennedy and Jacqueline Kennedy, who held a large bouquet of pink roses, standing a few feet away. The very second that Haile Selassie stepped out of the car, the herald trumpets of the military band sounded a blaring and glorious welcome. Black railroad porters stood watching all of this from behind the train—in amazement, it seemed to me—as official Washington greeted an African king. The emperor first shook President Kennedy's hand before turning to meet the First Lady, beautifully dressed in one of her signature pillbox hats and an Oleg Cassini suit. Her flawless French and dazzling grace put Haile Selassie immediately at ease. He then proceeded to move down the receiving line with Ambassador Duke making the introductions, all amidst a great exchange of pleasantries, high emotion, and the bobbing of heads. Watching the footage of these events today brings back to those of us old enough to remember it the great shock of President

Kennedy's assassination, which occurred only a few weeks after this state visit, which was one of the last of his administration. I felt this most acutely seeing film of the president and the emperor riding down a sun-dappled Pennsylvania Avenue in an open limousine, waving to smiling crowds on sidewalks bedecked in fluttering flags and royal crests, all beautifully choreographed.

After the parade, the emperor began a three-day whirlwind of speaking engagements and banquets, beginning with the chief justice's elegant luncheon aboard the *Sequoia*. A few hours later, having had time to refresh themselves, the official party gathered for the state dinner at the White House, the highest social occasion in Washington. The limousine carrying the emperor and Ambassador Duke arrived first. For this event, Haile Selassie wore his court uniform: an olive jacket, dark blue trousers, and myriad ribbons, medals, and gold braid. President Kennedy stood on the portico to greet him with his mother, Rose, who acted as hostess that evening in Jacqueline Kennedy's absence. The emperor's granddaughter, a princess, was in the second car, accompanied by Mrs. Duke. Altogether, 129 guests came to dinner that evening in shimmering formal dress. They ate with gold tableware and from china bought by Harry Truman. The only glitch, it seemed, showed up in the entertainment, a hapless dance troupe that performed a wild, 1920s-style ballet. From the president on down, nobody liked it, finding it inappropriate and risqué. I heard one U.S. official at the dinner say, "Well, we've just lost Ethiopia." But the emperor, serenely composed, said nothing, and clapped politely.

The next day, Secretary of State Dean Rusk hosted another sumptuous meal at the State Department, this one courtesy of a French caterer. While the White House had its own culinary staff, the State Department did not, so a caterer who could pass muster with the Secret Service got the job. Catering was, and still is, a major industry in Washington, and the telephone book lists more establishments than anyone can count; some are so exclusive they don't list their phone numbers. An assignment like this one was awarded to the lowest bidder, and caterers universally claimed that the events cost more than they were paid. But the jobs were coveted nonetheless for the cachet and public relations they provided.

The caterer selected for the Haile Selassie luncheon brought along a small army of staff, including an ice sculptor; at 7 a.m. they filed into the John Quincy Adams Room at the State Department and set to work. When this room was originally built, Congress refused to provide funds for crystal chandeliers, so C. Douglas Dillon, an undersecretary of state in the Eisenhower administration, and secretary of the treasury in Kennedy's, bought them with his own money because he felt strongly that official visitors should expect nothing less. Haile Selassie was to be served chicken Kiev that day, at a horseshoe table for 130 people. Throughout the morning, the actual number of guests fluctuated as last-minute cancellations and reversals were called in. Each time the head count changed, the table had to be reset to keep the proper distance between seats. This required a flurry of movements as all the china, silver, crystal, place cards, flowers, and salt and pepper shakers were rearranged. In those days, the State Department owned its china, emblazoned with the department seal, but chose to rent the caterer's silverware, because too many pieces of the department's collection had been pocketed as souvenirs. Out in the kitchen, the caterer nervously watched the clock and shouted orders in a mixture of languages; spoons were wiped clear of fingerprints, and glasses were set for three kinds of wine. Fifteen minutes before the guests' arrival at 1:30, Mrs. Rusk came in for an inspection, and pronounced everything perfect, much to the caterer's relief and delight.

While all this unfolded, the emperor was out and about in the capital. In a splendid scene that morning, he placed his wreath of solid silver at the Lincoln Memorial. The ceremony was stirring and somber, beginning with the emperor's ascension of the memorial steps between two cordons of American soldiers. In his arms he carried the glittering wreath, molded from 10,000 melted Ethiopian coins and inscribed with accolades to liberty—an impressive display for a man in his seventies, since the wreath must have weighed a ton. Stewart Udall, then secretary of the interior, led the emperor over to the side of the memorial where the Gettysburg Address, which Lincoln delivered in November 1863, is chiseled in five-inch letters, and where an interpreter read it as it had probably never been read before in Washington, in Amharic, the difficult native language of the emperor. Like everything else in official Washington that day, it was managed perfectly.

Next, it was off to the State Department,

where Haile Selassie held a news conference in a hall largely filled with U.S. government employees, to swell the crowd to
a size befitting royalty. Here he discussed
Ethiopia's border dispute with Somalia and
the goals of his five-year economic plan,
among other items. Everyone clapped as
he took leave of the podium for the eleva-
tor up to the Adams Room, where, as the
doors drew open, the view of a sparkling
dining room and the strains of the U.S.
Army Band string ensemble signaled the
beginning of another moment of theater,
carried off beautifully and without a hint
of tension.

On the third day, the emperor had to
leave, as agreed to in that meeting months
ago between Ambassadors Duke and
Dinke. But first, His Majesty had to fulfill
one of the requirements of protocol and
throw a few parties of his own, including
a luncheon for the president—which he
did—and a reception for diplomats and
various friends of his and Ethiopia's in
Washington. The Ethiopian embassy was
too small to accommodate the guest list of
one thousand, so the reception was moved
to a hotel. It turned out that 1,126 people
showed up, some of them the friends of
friends who held invitations, and other
party crashers, a social type peculiar to

Washington. These folks watch the papers to see who is having a big party, then put on their good clothes and walk right in. If the hosts try too hard to keep them out, there is the risk of making a mistake and insulting someone who is important. So all are accommodated.

The emperor and his party stood in yet another receiving line as the names of unknown persons were whispered into the ear of a protocol officer, who whispered them in turn to the senior diplomat's secretary, who whispered them to the Ethiopian ambassador, who then presented the guest to the emperor. Diplomats stood at the head of the line, and then everyone else, in no particular order. In his own country, Haile Selassie refused to shake hands; he required that people bow until they literally touched the floor, then slowly back away, facedown. Some of the women who knew how to curtsy did, but most did not because to Americans it is an alien custom. The official advice on that point still is, I believe, that unless you're an expert, don't try it, or you may wind up toppled on the carpet. I found this particular reception memorable for the comfort with which the very mixed crowd of black, brown, and white people socialized, sharing themselves in laughter and embrace.

This was 1963, after all, and outside the State Department, segregation reigned supreme in Washington, as it did across America. The party lacked for nothing in the way of food and drink, and when it was all over, it had cost the emperor $9,000 in 1963 dollars.

So in those three compressed days, Haile Selassie talked with President Kennedy about his dispute with Somalia and about his American aid; he went to two luncheons, a White House state dinner, and a reception; he threw a party; he laid a wreath and received an honorary degree from Georgetown University; he accepted the president's gifts—a replica of George Washington's sword and a movie projector; and he gave Mrs. Kennedy a leopard coat. When the appointed hour came, the emperor was driven by limousine to the Naval Observatory in the middle of town, where out on its rolling lawn state visitors left for the airport in a helicopter. The president did not come to see the emperor off, because the job of bidding official visitors adieu falls to the secretary of state. Once again the honor guard was assembled and the red carpet rolled out, and the emperor passed through a final receiving line of ambassadors and assorted officials as the herald trumpets blew a fanfare, hitting their climactic notes as he disappeared into the clouds. Thus the Lion of Judah flew away, finding it satisfactory to leave in a helicopter even though he had refused to arrive in one.

Does all this Byzantine ritual and splendor pay off? The answer seems to be a qualified yes, though if visitors from small, nervous countries discover that they have gotten a little less attention than some others—a shorter parade, a smaller dinner, fewer minutes with the president—they may go away furious. But if all goes well, as it did in this case, the visitor goes home a little closer friend than before he arrived. Haile Selassie flew from Washington to the United Nations in New York, where he said some extremely complimentary things about America, and until his house arrest in 1974 and his death in 1975 after a military coup, he remained America's staunch friend, a rarity in Cold War Africa.

Meanwhile the wheels of diplomacy grind on. As Emperor Haile Selassie vanished over the treetops that day, a man in downtown Washington started working on another banner to be hung from fire ladders across Pennsylvania Avenue. It read: WELCOME TO THE PRIME MINISTER OF IRELAND.

The Kennedy Assassination

Just as almost all Americans alive today will certainly recall what they were doing when they heard the news of the catastrophic events of September 11, 2001, all of us old enough surely remember where we were when the news came that President John Kennedy had been shot. I was in my office at the NBC Washington bureau on Nebraska Avenue that Friday, trying to decide what news we had that was worth using on the air that night. On that day, the president was in Texas at the urging of Vice President Lyndon Johnson, to do a little politicking in Johnson's home state. Johnson and Governor John Connally were escorting him around. Kennedy then was a little less than a year away from the next presidential election, and because he had almost lost Texas in 1960, a quick swing through the state looked to be worth the trip, so much so, in fact, that he did what he almost never did on campaign tours: persuaded his wife to go with him.

In the early afternoon, as I and the other NBC people were coming back from lunch, looking over the day's wire service stories, and seeing there was not much other news, we were talking about starting the program that night with the Kennedy trip to Texas. At almost that moment, Robert MacNeil, the Canadian-born NBC correspondent who later became the respected cohost of the *MacNeil/Lehrer NewsHour* on PBS, was riding in the motorcade through Dallas with the president and heard what he thought were gunshots. Like most of the other reporters, though, he could not get to a phone. The first news from Dallas came from Merriman Smith of United Press International, who was riding in a car that was equipped with a built-in telephone. Since no one yet knew what was happening, the first reports stated simply that "shots were fired" near the presidential motorcade. A few minutes later, the astonishing story, one of the shortest ever wired: "JFK shot." That was how we in Washington heard the news.

In newsrooms everywhere, there was frenzied scrambling as we tried to find out what had happened. Chet Huntley, who worked out of New York, rushed into the

New York studio, along with Bill Ryan and Frank McGee, while I hurried into the Washington one to give what little news there was. But the very first announcement broadcast on NBC came not from any of our newsmen, but from staff announcer Don Pardo (later famous as the announcer on *Jeopardy!* and *Saturday Night Live*), who was the first to find an open microphone. Voice trembling, he came on the national network from New York at 1:45:03 p.m. eastern standard time and said, "President Kennedy was shot in Dallas, Texas, today. Blood was seen on the president's head as they rushed him to a hospital. Mrs. Kennedy was heard to exclaim, 'Oh, no.'"

It took another minute and forty-two seconds to get the network switched together at an hour of day when normally stations are carrying local programs. In Washington, I noticed that our local affiliate, WRC-TV, was broadcasting some kind of fashion show. To make it worse, those whose authorization was necessary to shift to the national network were out to lunch. For a time, all we could do was sit there and watch models strutting down a catwalk.

Finally, the network cut in and took over the air. In NBC's primitive little New

York studio, Ryan, Huntley, and McGee scrambled to relay the fragments of information we had. They were jammed into what we called the "flash studio," which was about the size of a large closet and had only one black-and-white camera. I was crammed into another tiny space in Washington. For a while, there was almost nothing we could do but keep rereading the same wire service dispatches, which simply repeated themselves over and over again.

The president, the vice president, the governor of Texas, and their families were all in Parkland Memorial Hospital, where doctors were working frantically on the president, realizing all along that there was nothing they could do for him. But outside the hospital, no one knew what was happening. Even the White House press staff in Texas was in chaos, not yet sure what was going on.

The first reports said that Kennedy and Connally, who had also been shot, were still alive. Some priests were brought to the hospital—obviously for the president, since Connally was not a Catholic—but we were told that they were there just as a "precaution." That was all we knew, and we did not want to alarm the audience by saying more. For forty-five long, tortured minutes, all we heard was that Kennedy's condition was "uncertain."

MacNeil by now was on a pay phone in the hospital, feeding what little he knew directly to Frank McGee. We were unable to patch MacNeil directly onto the air because of overloaded circuits, so McGee had to hold the phone to his ear and repeat what MacNeil reported, sentence by sentence. When MacNeil had to leave the phone to get the latest news, he had a medical student keep the line open.

In those years, our technical facilities were still pretty undeveloped. Without satellites, we could not send pictures across the continent instantaneously. Bill Ryan in New York had to hold up in front of the camera AP still photos of the motorcade going through Dallas. At one point, we tried to switch to WBAP, our affiliate in Fort Worth, for a report, but all we got was feedback, a soul-stirring, high-pitched screech caused by electrons running into one another. Ryan maintained his composure and explained on the air that "this is a time of what would probably best be described as controlled panic," and that the noise from Fort Worth occurred "under conditions of extreme pressure."

Twenty minutes into the broadcast they switched to me for "the Washington reaction" to the news. At that time, there wasn't much to report. Most people I heard from were in shock, waiting to hear whether John Kennedy would survive. All I could do was report that the president's brother, Ted Kennedy, was presiding over the Senate for a time, and was informed of the terrible news by majority leader Mike Mansfield, who whispered in his ear. Kennedy said nothing but laid down the gavel and walked out of the Senate chamber. Later I reported that Congress had adjourned for the day; that four of the president's cabinet members had been on a plane headed for Japan. It had turned around over the Pacific and headed back to Washington. An orchestral concert in Constitution Hall was in progress that afternoon. The conductor returned to the stage during an ovation, told the audience that the president had been shot, and said above their cries and gasps that he prayed the reports were not true.

All over the city, people were telling one another what news they had, and the whole atmosphere was hushed and somehow eerie. Church bells were ringing hopefully everywhere.

About a half hour into our broadcast, the news grew increasingly grim. First, at 2:33 p.m., Bill Ryan read an AP flash reporting that the priests who had seen the president were saying that he was dead. A minute later, McGee said that Lyndon Johnson had been rushed out of the hospital, although we did not yet know where he was going. And at 2:36 p.m., Frank McGee finally relayed the shattering official news from MacNeil: the president of the United States was dead.

When I first met John F. Kennedy in about 1947, he was a newly elected and almost unknown member of Congress—frail-looking, vaguely jaundiced, and widely assumed to be recovering from injuries and tropical diseases he had contracted during the war. As became known later, he was suffering from a variety of serious health problems that had been with him all his life and would remain with him until he died. There was little about him at the time to suggest that he had presidential stature and presence, let alone that he was a man who would occupy a place of mythic importance in American history. He was attractive and charming, and he seemed reasonably intelligent; but what most people wondered about was his wealthy, powerful father, Joe Kennedy, who was not much liked by many. We underestimated

him. John Kennedy was a survivor. He
had survived a series of terrible illnesses
when he was young. He had survived a
Japanese torpedo during the war. He survived, and largely overcame, the unsavory
reputation of his father and established
himself in the 1950s as a fresh young face
in the Democratic Party. And in 1960,
during the Democratic primaries, he even
managed to survive being a Catholic candidate for president, as no one had done
since Al Smith won the nomination in
1928 and then lost disastrously to Herbert
Hoover.

I first began to take Kennedy seriously
when I went to West Virginia to cover
its Democratic primary for NBC in the
spring of 1960. I was particularly interested
in how Protestant coal miners in that
poor state would respond to a member of
a wealthy Catholic family from Boston.
What I found was deep anger at the coal
companies that had dug out the state's natural wealth and sold the coal all over the
world, leaving nothing behind but poverty
and ugly holes in the ground. Many West
Virginians liked Kennedy just because he
was young and new and did not look
like the newspaper-cartoon politicians
they knew and largely despised. Still, in
the weeks before the primary, Kennedy

seemed to be in trouble. The polls showed him losing to Hubert Humphrey, one of the more appealing members of the Democratic leadership, and the only other serious contender in the West Virginia primary. There were stories, some probably true, that Kennedy's father was spreading money around the state—a state where it was said a vote could be bought for a half-pint of cheap whiskey.

But Kennedy worked hard, spoke carefully, promised he would not let the pope dictate to him, and appealed to voters not to allow their religious views to affect their votes. It came to seem that the only way to avoid appearing bigoted was to vote for Kennedy. Whether because of his campaigning skills, or his father's money, or both, the religious issue went away and he won the primary and went on to defeat Richard Nixon narrowly in the fall election.

I was never an intimate of Kennedy's, but I always liked him. Most reporters in Washington knew the stories about his sexual philandering in his Senate days, but not until later did I become aware of how extensive and almost pathological it was. At the time, though, few of us cared much about that. As it is said, more or less accurately, most of them do it and so Kennedy was hardly alone among politicians with a thirst for power who exercised it in any available bedroom. It seemed irrelevant to his ability to govern. Some in the press, which was nearly all male, may have secretly envied his talents.

In any case, Kennedy was famously popular with the press in a way that no politician is today. He treated us like friends and, at times, almost like secret co-conspirators, flattering reporters by confiding in them, but always in a way that served his own interests. The Washington press corps was not as cynical then as it is now, and many were seduced by the president's wit and charm. He once telephoned me at home to thank me for saying on the air that we would no longer show his young children on television because we thought that they, like other children, were entitled to privacy. Even though I knew it was a calculated gesture, I was pleased.

He also became a great and effective media figure. He was the first president to arrive and grow up in the age of television, and he was the first who knew how to use it. He moved his press conferences out of the dark, Victorian Indian Treaty Room in the Old Executive Office Building next door to the White House and into the sleek, modern State Department auditorium a few blocks away. And they were great television events. He fielded most questions quickly and effectively, but in some ways he was almost better when he was stumped because he always came up with a neat little joke to get himself out of trouble. He was especially impressive after the dry, barren press conferences of Eisenhower, who once told his press secretary he would deliberately give answers so convoluted and obscure that the reporters would not be able to figure out what he had said, if anything. So the press—most of it—loved Kennedy.

It astonished me sometimes to see the kind of passion Kennedy could unleash, and I think it must have astonished him too. Some of it was a desperate and unreasoning hatred, most of it coming from the political right. It was probably not as intense as the right-wing hatred Franklin Roosevelt and Bill Clinton attracted, but it was substantial. And it never stopped. But even more intense was the adulation he received and the excitement he generated. None of it ever seemed to bother him much.

In truth, Kennedy was a cool, somewhat detached figure who appeared to have little ideological passion of his own. But to much of the American public, and maybe

even more to the rest of the world, wherever they paid attention, he was seen in the
superheated atmosphere of the Cold War
to be a fervent crusader. In Berlin in 1963,
he received a welcome larger and warmer
than any American president had seen in
Europe since Woodrow Wilson went to
Paris after World War I. One reason
Kennedy's death was so traumatic to people all over the world was that so many of
them had already begun to idolize him
while he was alive.

What I and others most liked about him
was what came to be called his pragmatism. Unlike some of the New Dealers of
the 1930s, who continued to push their
ideas even after they had become clear fail-
ures, Kennedy surrounded himself with
advisors who thought an idea was good
only if it worked. If a program or a law or
an agency was found to serve no useful
purpose, they had no interest in defending
it. Those in his administration thought the
purpose of government was to solve problems and correct social wrongs, but they
were just as concerned with what was possible. To them, an idea was good only if it
could be used efficiently and with not too
much controversy or discord. Being dog-
matic and asking too much of Congress,
the real center of power in the govern-

ment, either alienated potential allies or made it more difficult to get anything done at all. Sometimes this pragmatism could look like an excuse for timidity. At first, Kennedy was slow and reluctant, for example, to support the growing civil rights movement, afraid it would undermine his standing with southerners in Congress. But in 1963, when the movement had become too large to ignore, he put himself fully and forcefully behind it.

He was especially good at choosing cabinet members and advisors. He surrounded himself with people who were young and energetic, but careful and unemotional, intellectual and sober. His cabinet may have been one of the most talented in modern times. They were, to use a phrase that later became one of derision, "the best and the brightest." Looking back today, it's clear that Kennedy's men (and they were all men) were not just bright, but often arrogant; that their confidence in themselves could lead them into trouble. Consider Kennedy's failed attempts to overthrow Cuba's Fidel Castro: a disaster. The effort to defeat the Communists in Vietnam: an even greater catastrophe. At the time, however, all that was clear was that the power was now in the hands of people of youth and energy and humor, most of it coming from the White House.

All that ended even more abruptly than it had begun.

As the news that Kennedy had been murdered began to sink in, many people in the government, and many in the press, had trouble keeping their emotions under control. That made it hard to report the news accurately and professionally. Huntley and McGee in New York were visibly upset and clearly nervous on camera. They were both chain-smoking, and the smoke from their cigarettes was visible on the air, normally against NBC rules. Martin Agronsky, my colleague in the Washington bureau, choked up, unable to talk for a minute or two. Bill Ryan kept a steady manner but looked grave and uncertain. I managed to keep my composure as well.

For a while after the terrible news, there was not much to report. About the only visual images we had to put on the air were scenes of the crowds gathered across the street from the White House, standing quietly around in Lafayette Park in cloudy, chilly weather, simply looking at the curtained windows, because they couldn't think of anything else to do. We worried for a time about the lack of news and the repetition of our few strands of information. But I now believe that a little quiet time on televisions across the country was important to the American people, that it helped prevent the spread of poisonous rumors. They were the secondary victims of a historic crime, stunned by its suddenness and finality, left to wonder uneasily what it meant, whether our national stability was in danger. It was the ultimate crime in a country already worried about growing criminality, already locking its doors at night and hesitating to use the streets after dark. No one yet knew who had shot the president or why, whether whoever it was had other killings planned. In the first confused hours, there were rumors that Lyndon Johnson, now president, had also been shot, and a story that he had had a heart attack. The situation could have led to panic or mass hysteria, and we consoled ourselves by speculating that we could reassure people by offering them calm and familiar faces and voices in this time of anxiety and uncertainty.

We were not really much better informed than anyone else. Rumors about the culprits flooded in from every direction. The Soviet news agency was report-

ing as fact that American right-wing cra-
zies had killed the president, while others,
knowing nothing, claimed that this was
part of a plot by the Soviet Union. In one
version, the Soviets, with the help of Fidel
Castro and Cuba, were all together in a
plan to overthrow the United States government. Several people we interviewed
on the street thought that southern segregationists or radical isolationists had arranged it, rumors that seemed credible to
some because Adlai Stevenson, the U.S.
ambassador to the United Nations, had recently been attacked and spat upon during
a visit to Dallas.

Finally, a rumor turned out to have some
substance. At 2:30 p.m. we heard that a
suspect had been arrested after killing a police officer on the street. The suspect turned out to be Lee Harvey Oswald.
He was charged with firing a rifle at the
president from an upstairs window in the
Texas School Book Depository.

Even through all this, we had to think
about the beginning of a new administration and a new president. Shortly after we
heard that Kennedy had died, I went on
the air to explain how the system worked
for the few who did not know, and to say
that Vice President Johnson was now president. I didn't realize that he had already

been sworn in aboard the president's airplane. It had been eighteen years since another president had died in office, peacefully, in Warm Springs, Georgia.

For a time, then, the new president was nowhere to be seen. Because there was great uncertainty about what had happened, and because there were fears that the assassination might be part of a larger conspiracy, Johnson had been completely hidden from public view since the shooting. As soon as they could, the Secret Service took him to Air Force One, the plane on which President Kennedy had arrived in Dallas earlier. His bodyguards thought that was the safest place at the moment. And Johnson had taken the oath of office from a Texas judge, a friend of his, standing in the airplane and holding up his right hand. There with him was Mrs. Kennedy, still wearing a pink suit stained with her husband's blood. Despite her great reluctance, she had been persuaded to stand beside the new president as a symbol of the continuity of government.

None of this was visible to anyone outside the plane until the White House released a grainy photograph of the ceremony, the least stately picture of a presidential oath-taking in American history—all the participants standing cramped together in a small airplane cabin. They then took off for Washington, carrying the new president and the casket of his predecessor.

A chartered Boeing 707 full of NBC newsmen and technicians heading from New York to Dallas was diverted to Washington. By the time Air Force One and the NBC plane got there, all the flags in the city were at half-mast and the transition to a new presidential administration was already under way. Martin Agronsky reported that Kennedy's secretary was removing mementos from his desk—the family pictures, the PT-109 souvenirs. There was even news film of Kennedy's famous rocking chair being wheeled out of the White House. (Many people were appalled at this public display of a private event, and some blamed Johnson, who knew nothing about it.) A woman from Minnesota wrote to me a day later, showing how high passions were running: "Texas killed him: must Texas now humiliate him?"

That night, after all the news had gone out around the world, Edwin Newman, one of our best writers, ruminated on the air:

The unpleasant truth about America is that it is a country of violence. Violence plays a part in our very lives—yet what we worry about is our image abroad. Today, America does not appear to be an adult country. Emotions run high— regional, religious, and economic. We must begin at the top, for the political climate is set by the president. In the days to come we will hear much of how we must stick together. It is within our power to take our public life more seriously than we have. Americans tonight are a grossly diminished people.

Sander Vanocur, our White House correspondent, who had rushed back from a vacation to cover the story, was more hopeful. He expressed his faith in the power of the presidency and in the American political system. He assured his viewers that an orderly continuation of government under Lyndon Johnson would take place now and the republic would not fall because of an act of terror.

I agreed with him, but felt called to add, "If we have come to the point where a president cannot appear in public without fear of being shot, then we are less civilized than we think we are." And at the end of our broadcast that night, I tried to sum up:

About all that could happen has happened. It is one of the ugliest days in American history. There is seldom any time to think anymore, and today there was none. In about four hours we had gone from President Kennedy in Dallas, alive, to back in Washington, dead, and a new president in his place. There is really no more to say except that what happened has been just too much, too ugly, and too fast.

But there was, of course, still another twist in this awful story less than two days later. Lee Harvey Oswald had been brought into the Dallas police headquarters after his arrest and was soon identified as the main suspect. On Sunday morning he was scheduled to be transferred from the city jail to the county jail—which was more secure, they said. There were rumors through the night of death threats against Oswald sent to the FBI and the Dallas police. After being scooped on the assassination, NBC's producers made sure that we were ready for any dramatic turn of events in Dallas. One of our executives suspected that something might happen when they moved Oswald. We put cameras at both jails hours before the transfer. When our reporter in Dallas signaled that Oswald was coming out of the city jail, even though in Washington the caisson carrying the president's coffin was moving up Pennsylvania Avenue before enormous throngs crowding the street, we cut to live coverage in Dallas just as the doors of the jail opened. NBC got the first-ever live television picture of a murder. Jack Ruby, a Dallas nightclub owner, stepped forward with a pistol and fired a single, fatal, pistol shot into Oswald's ribs. Our reporter shouted, "He's been shot! He's been shot! Lee Harvey Oswald has been shot!" The other networks broadcast our film.

Of course there were critics. A woman in Florida wrote to me: "At a time when the nation is in a state of shock from an unbelievable tragedy, we are faced with endless hours of the nightmare being repeated over and over again." But I thought then, and think now, that since all of us on the networks stayed with it until the last, we helped the American people get through a sad and scary time by showing and telling everything there was to show and tell, by preventing the spread of the frightening rumors, by showing people that even in so horrible a time orderly government continued, and by giving the new president a way to speak reassuring words to a people who desperately needed them. In my opinion, it was the most useful single service in television's history.

Would we have covered that tragic weekend any differently today? Not much, I think. Our journalistic judgment then was that the time called for calm and unexcited exposition of all the events and facts available to us, delivered without histrionics or emotional outbursts—particularly as some of the same doubts and fears that occupied the public also occupied us in the first hours and days: Was the government in danger? Were there threats to other leaders? Was some force or entity, foreign or domestic, involved in this? If so, who and why? Not all the answers were available in those first hours and days, but the questions were there. And it seemed essential to us that we tell the public everything we knew and show them everything there was to see.

That was what we did, all of us on all the networks, and while it was impossible to make sense of the senseless, I do think we helped persuade a doubting, skeptical, fearful people that they were being told everything we knew at the time. In the same circumstances today, God forbid, I would see no reason to do it any other way.

Technically, of course, we could perform better now. For instance, nobody started recording until eleven minutes into the broadcast, so some important visual history was lost. There were delays for film processing and editing, since there was not yet magnetic videotape. The cameras were bigger and heavier and more difficult to move and set up than they are now. Getting the news out was just a slower, more laborious process than it is today.

But I doubt even the many improvements since then would make a great deal of difference. The higher speeds are helpful in day-to-day news programs with rigid deadlines. A foreign report we once had to fly across the Atlantic for use on Tuesday night would now be sent by satellite to be broadcast on Monday night, and even live if the times were right. But on a continuous, live program like the Kennedy death and funeral, speed was not so much a factor. It was nearly all live.

Edwin Newman said that television "came of age" on that day. The American people saw, after the first stunning shock, that our national structure went on, that the solemn formalities were carried out with efficiency and care and taste, right down to the folding of the American flag into a triangle. It was a shared experience unlike any other because we could all see it and hear it. People grieving in private witnessed others grieving in public. And I doubt that many who saw it will forget the image of John Jr.—who years later would himself die tragically and prematurely—saluting his father's coffin.

Until the day Kennedy died, the television networks were secondary sources of information for most of the public. People relied on radio and newspapers to get their news. But the assassination changed all that. The Nielsen company reported that 96 percent of the country's households tuned in to one of the networks for coverage of the assassination. According to Nielsen, the average television viewer watched an astounding nine hours a day over the weekend. It was our first genuinely national funeral, a death in all our families, a funeral attended by everyone.

Since that time, the American people have been treated to an outpouring of speculation by pundits, historians, filmmakers, and cranks about what happened on November 22, 1963. For forty years, hundreds of books and articles have attempted to reveal the real truth about the murder, who really did the shooting and why, who put him up to it, what foreign country or American institution was behind it, and on and on. Oliver Stone's movie *JFK* offered a ridiculous account of a murder plotted and executed by the Mafia, the CIA, and an assortment of mysterious right–wing characters from around the world.

Some tried to show that he was a peacemonger, killed because he tried to pull out of Vietnam. The truth is that Kennedy was one of the most devoted militarists in presidential history. In the 1960 campaign he denounced Eisenhower for allowing the Soviet Union to build more long-range missiles than we had, calling it a "missile gap." The charges were untrue. Once in office, he built up the military faster than any peacetime president before him. A few months before he died, he approved a plot by a group of South Vietnamese generals to overthrow President Ngo Dinh Diem, who was later murdered along with his brother. The Kennedy administration wanted Diem out because he was not waging the war as effectively as they thought he should. Kennedy said, "I don't agree with those who say we should withdraw.

That would be a great mistake." There was a mistake, but it was Kennedy's.

As the years have passed and much else has happened, good and bad, and as we look back on the incredible sight on live television of a man climbing out of a spacecraft onto the surface of the moon, it is interesting to recall Kennedy's final speech, written but never delivered. It included a promise to press on with exploring space and landing on the moon. But in the last speech he actually delivered, in Fort Worth the morning before he died, he said something that seems as apt for our time as it did for his: "We would like to live as we once lived, but history will not permit it. . . . We are still the keystone in the arch of freedom. And I think we will continue to do as we have done in the past—our duty."

Those were his last public words before a weekend none of us can ever forget and none of us will ever fully understand, a weekend when I was sorry for our country, but also proud of television for helping us all to see the sights of tragedy and then to go on.

A Reflection on a Life
in Broadcast News

When they found how to connect the tubes and wires together and to send pictures through the air, out came a new creature called the anchorman. God knows where that term originated. Some of us who have held the position have never liked it, but there it is. Having spent a good part of my career as an anchorman—for about twenty years, off and on, at NBC on the nightly news, most of them with Chet Huntley; and then for another fifteen years at ABC on a Sunday morning show—I've had plenty of time to think about the role of the anchorman (and now, occasionally, anchorwoman).

That role is difficult to assess, because there is nothing to compare to it. Newspaper reporters or editors do some of the same kinds of work, but they are not more or less personally in the living room every night and are not instantly recognizable in

airports, pool rooms, and saloons. A newspaper reporter has to spell it. An anchor
has to pronounce it.

But the great difference, I think, is that
in a night-to-night or day-to-day relationship with tens of millions of people, including those with TV sets in living
rooms, bedrooms, and poolside cabanas,
the anchorman gives the news a kind of
dimension and character it never had before, mediated through his own voice and
appearance and personality. The news then
becomes not just what happened but what
a familiar face and voice says happened,
and the meaning of it is to some extent determined by how he says it.

It is quite a strange relationship, and only
a few people have experienced it in the
roughly half century since television news
became a significant force in American life.
Even now, having spent most of my adult
life in the role, I am unable to define it precisely, or even to describe it. Between the
anchorman and the audience, there is a
kind of intimate remoteness. They know
his clothes and his haircuts and to some extent his likes and dislikes. They watch him
get older. They feel they know him, and in
a way they do. But he does not know them.

By now, it has become accepted as journalism. But it bears only a scant relationship

to the journalism we knew in the past—and still know in media other than broadcasting. In the end, television news is not merely the same news delivered in a different way. Because the means of its delivery changes its meaning to its audience—through its immediacy, through its connection to personalities, and through the inevitable superficiality created by the medium's time constraints. It is also different from other kinds of news because it reaches more, and different, people, many of them barely, if at all, reached by other news.

It might be politically dangerous for any one person to have that much access to so many eyes and ears. It is worth remembering that the world's first important television personality was Adolf Hitler. In prewar Germany, he harangued people over the crude television sets that Germans placed in bars and other public places long before Americans did. But as our own politicians have lately discovered, the American people tend to believe little of what they hear from their government; they tend to assume that whatever they are told by political leaders is a pack of lies. And as we have seen, and continue to see, remarkably often they are right. To some degree, the same is true of journalists, and television journalists in particular. Deliver-

ing the news on television is not unlike appearing on the stage of a provincial Italian
opera house. When the aria is over, nobody
knows if the reaction will be cheers and applause, or cabbage and tomatoes, or both.

In my view, television news tends more
to reinforce the existing social and political
values than to change them, and the recur-
ring cry that it and other news media excessively influence public opinion in one
political direction or another seems to me
an empty claim. It must be if, after a half
century of news reporting that has been
regularly charged with being excessively
liberal, we have recently elected some of
our most conservative presidents.

TV newspeople serve the useful public
function of delivering the goods, attrac-
tively wrapped, in the hope of attracting
some millions of people to tune in. In recent decades, I fear, the wrapping has sometimes become too attractive—indeed, has
sometimes almost obscured what is inside—
and much television news, in response to
economic pressures, competition, and perhaps a basic lack of commitment to the in-
tegrity and value of the enterprise, has
become so trivial and devoid of content as
to be little different from entertainment
programming. But even at its best, television news is driven less by the ideology of

those who deliver it than by the pressures of the medium itself. And as a result, individual journalists, from the anchors to the local news-beat reporters, are all constrained in their power by the skepticism of a public that from the beginning saw in television something closer to the tradition of entertainment (movies, theater, and the like) than to the tradition of the press.

The television journalist does have the power to steer the public's attention in one direction or another. He can make an obscure person famous for a day or two, but not much longer than that unless the person is then able to hold the public's attention with his own resources. It can keep a story alive for weeks, even months, but it cannot ensure that the public will continue to believe in it. The year or more during which the news media was obsessed with the Monica Lewinsky scandal, for example, saw a significant rise in President Clinton's public approval ratings and a significant decline in the media's.

There is no question that television journalists, and particularly television anchors, have become enormously famous. Most of my adult life has been shaped by that reality. But I do not believe that I, or my fellow anchors, have become famous for our power to influence uncritical masses of people, or for our ability to change the social or political order or to elect a candidate or defeat one. So what are we famous for? Mainly, we are famous for being famous.

To survive, an anchor must convince some millions of people that he is at least modestly competent, that he has some idea of what he is talking about, and that he is playing straight with them, and that is about all. He might comb his hair if he has any (and virtually all anchors have quite a lot) and wear a tie and keep his suits pressed. But people seem not to care too much whether or not he is attractive or well groomed, so long as he delivers the goods in a way they consider capable and honest.

I believe that all of the network anchors of my time—Ed Murrow, Walter Cronkite, Dan Rather, Howard K. Smith, Barbara Walters, Frank Reynolds, Peter Jennings, John Chancellor, Tom Brokaw, my longtime partner Chet Huntley, and the rest—have done that pretty well, and I tried to do the same. But is there any real power? I believe not. Over the years, several television newsmen, not understanding that they were famous only for being famous, have run for political office. Most of them lost.

Note About the Author

DAVID BRINKLEY was born in Wilmington, North Carolina. After his army service in the 1940s, he worked for United Press and then joined NBC, where he launched *The Huntley-Brinkley Report* with Chet Huntley in 1956. He was also coanchor of the *NBC Nightly News* with John Chancellor and hosted ABC's *This Week with David Brinkley.* He was the recipient of ten Emmy Awards and three George Foster Peabody Awards. He died in June 2003.